GAO
Accountability · Integrity · Reliability

Highlights

Highlights of GAO-12-86, a report to congressional requesters

October 2011

DEEPWATER HORIZON OIL SPILL

Actions Needed to Reduce Evolving but Uncertain Federal Financial Risks

Why GAO Did This Study

On April 20, 2010, an explosion of the *Deepwater Horizon* oil rig leased by BP America Production Company (BP) resulted in a significant oil spill. GAO was requested to (1) identify the financial risks to the federal government resulting from oil spills, particularly *Deepwater Horizon,* (2) assess the Coast Guard's internal controls for ensuring that processes and payments for spill-related cost reimbursements and claims related to the spill are appropriate, and (3) describe the extent to which the federal government oversees the BP and Gulf Coast Claims Facility cost reimbursement and claims processes. We issued status reports in November 2010 and April 2011. This is the third and final report related to these objectives. We obtained and analyzed data on costs incurred from April 2010 through May 2011 and claims submitted and processed from September 2010 through May 2011. We reviewed relevant policies and procedures, interviewed officials and staff at key federal departments and agencies, and tested a sample of claims processed and cost reimbursements paid for compliance with internal controls.

What GAO Recommends

GAO is (1) reiterating that Congress may want to consider setting a Fund cap per incident based upon net expenditures, (2) presenting a new matter concerning extending the barrel tax used to finance federal oil spill responses to sustain program funding, and (3) making a recommendation to improve procedures for future significant spills. In responding, the Department of Homeland Security concurred with the recommendation.

View GAO-12-86 or key components. For more information, contact Susan Ragland at (202) 512-8486 or raglands@gao.gov.

What GAO Found

Both the individual circumstances of the *Deepwater Horizon* incident, as well as the overall framework for how the federal government responds to oil spills, present a mix of evolving, but as yet uncertain, financial risks to the federal government and its Oil Spill Liability Trust Fund (Fund). The extent of financial risks to the federal government from the *Deepwater Horizon* is closely tied to BP and the other responsible parties. BP established a $20 billion Trust to pay for individual and business claims and other expenses. As of May 31, 2011, BP has paid over $700 million of federal and state government costs for oil spill cleanup. Federal agency cleanup and restoration activities are under way and agencies continue to incur costs and submit them for reimbursement. However, the full extent of these costs, particularly those related to environmental cleanup, may not be fully realized for some time. As cleanup costs continue to mount, it is possible that expenditures from the Fund will reach the $1 billion total expenditure per incident cap. Expenditures were over $626 million on May 31, 2011. If these amounts reach the total expenditure cap of $1 billion, the Fund can no longer be used to make payments to reimburse agencies' costs (or to pay valid individual or business claims if not paid by the responsible parties). At that point, government agencies would no longer be able to obtain reimbursement for their costs. In November 2010, GAO suggested that Congress may want to consider setting a Fund per incident cap based on net expenditures (expenditures less reimbursement), rather than total expenditures. Finally, GAO found the federal government's longer-term ability to provide financial support in response to future oil spills is also at risk because the Fund's primary source of revenue, a tax on petroleum products, is scheduled to expire in 2017.

GAO's testing of the Coast Guard's internal controls over *Deepwater Horizon* claims processed and cost reimbursements processed and paid showed that adjudicated claims processed and costs reimbursed were appropriate and properly documented. In November 2010, GAO made four recommendations regarding establishing and maintaining effective cost reimbursement policies and procedures for the Fund. The Coast Guard changed its operating practices to reflect lessons learned from the initial response to the *Deepwater Horizon* incident, and it has updated its cost reimbursement procedures accordingly. However, the Coast Guard has not yet updated its procedures for processing significant claims, so lessons learned from its experiences processing *Deepwater Horizon* claims could be lost. Capturing lessons learned about processing such claims will be essential should a significant spill occur in the future.

The federal government has used a variety of approaches to oversee BP's and GCCF's cost reimbursement and claims processing. Soon after the *Deepwater Horizon* oil spill, the federal government established a Deepwater Integrated Services Team (IST), which was initially responsible for monitoring BP's claims process, among other things. Subsequently, the oversight of cost reimbursement and claims activities transitioned to the Department of Justice, which continues to lead this and other efforts. In addition, the Department of the Interior and the National Oceanic and Atmospheric Administration are serving as the federal government's representatives for the natural resource trustees in evaluating the environmental impact of the *Deepwater Horizon* spill and selecting and implementing restoration projects to be funded by BP.

_____ United States Government Accountability Office

Contents

Abbreviations

BP	BP American Production Company
COFR	Certificate of Financial Responsibility
DHS	Department of Homeland Security
DOD	Department of Defense
DOI	Department of the Interior
EPA	Environmental Protection Agency
FEMA	Federal Emergency Management Agency
FINCEN	Coast Guard's Finance Center
FOSC	Federal On-Scene Coordinator
GCCF	Gulf Coast Claims Facility
IG	inspector general
IST	Integrated Services Team
MIPR	Military Interdepartmental Purchase Request
NOAA	National Oceanic and Atmospheric Administration
NPFC	National Pollution Funds Center
OMB	Office of Management and Budget
OPA	Oil Pollution Act of 1990, as amended
PRFA	Pollution Removal Funding Authorization

United States Government Accountability Office
Washington, DC 20548

October 24, 2011

Congressional Requesters

The explosion on the BP America Production Company's (BP) leased *Deepwater Horizon* oil rig in the Gulf of Mexico on April 20, 2010 resulted in one of the largest environmental disasters in U.S. history.[1] Along with the devastating environmental impact, the *Deepwater Horizon* oil spill affected the livelihoods of thousands of Gulf Coast citizens and businesses. The total costs to clean up this unprecedented spill, ease the economic suffering of affected parties in the region, and assess and mitigate its eventual environmental impact remain unknown but have been estimated in the tens of billions of dollars.

The Oil Pollution Act of 1990, as amended (OPA), which was enacted after the *Exxon Valdez* oil spill in 1989, established a "polluter pays" system that places the primary burden of liability for costs of spills up to a statutory maximum, on the responsible parties—BP and several other companies in this case.[2] However, responsible parties are liable without limit if the oil discharge is the result of gross negligence or willful misconduct, or a violation of federal operation, safety, and construction regulations. OPA provides the Oil Spill Liability Trust Fund (Fund) to pay for oil spill costs when the responsible party cannot or does not pay. The Fund is administered by the Coast Guard through its National Pollution Funds Center (NPFC), is primarily financed through a tax on petroleum products, and is subject to a $1 billion cap on the amount of expenditures

---

[1]BP America Production Company, a subsidiary of BP p.l.c., leased the *Deepwater Horizon* from Transocean Holdings LLC, a subsidiary of Transocean Limited. Transocean Limited is the world's largest offshore drilling contractor comprising numerous subsidiaries and jointly controlled entities and associates. Unless otherwise referring to specific subsidiaries or affiliates, we refer to Transocean Limited and its components separately or jointly as "Transocean." BP p.l.c. is an international oil and gas company comprising numerous subsidiaries and jointly controlled entities and associates. Unless otherwise referring to specific subsidiaries or affiliates, we refer to BP p.l.c. and its components separately or jointly as "BP." BP was originally incorporated in 1909 in England and Wales as "British Petroleum" and changed its name in 2001.

[2]Pub. L. No. 101-380, 104 Stat. 484 (Aug. 18, 1990).The Coast Guard identified the following companies as responsible parties or guarantors for the *Deepwater Horizon* oil spill: BP Exploration & Production, Inc.; BP Corporation North America, Inc.; Anardarko, E&P Company, LP; Anardarko Petroleum Corporation; MOEX Offshore 2007 LLC; Transocean Holdings Incorporated; and QBE Underwriting, LTD.

from the Fund per incident.[3] NPFC administers the Fund by disbursing funds to government agencies to reimburse them for their oil spill cleanup costs (cost reimbursements), monitoring the sources and uses of funds, adjudicating claims submitted by individuals and businesses to the Fund for payment (claims), and pursuing reimbursement from the responsible party for costs and damages paid from the Fund (billing the responsible party).

In the case of the *Deepwater Horizon* oil spill, BP, as well as others, have been identified as responsible parties. In this capacity, BP established multiple claims centers along the Gulf Coast to receive and process individuals' and businesses' damage claims; on May 3, 2010, BP began paying emergency compensation to them. In June 2010, as part of an oral agreement between the Obama Administration and BP, BP established a new claims processing facility, the Gulf Coast Claims Facility (GCCF). GCCF, administered by Kenneth Feinberg, began operations on August 23, 2010, and is responsible for handling claims from individuals and businesses for damages resulting from the spill. BP also established an irrevocable trust in August 2010—primarily to pay claims approved by GCCF among other purposes—and pledged to incrementally provide a total of $20 billion to the trust by 2014.[4]

Shortly after the April 20, 2010 explosion, members of Congress requested that we (1) identify the financial risks to the federal government resulting from oil spills, particularly *Deepwater Horizon*, (2) assess NPFC's internal controls for ensuring that processes and payments for cost reimbursements and processes for claims related to the *Deepwater Horizon* spill were appropriate, and (3) describe the extent to which the federal government oversees the BP and GCCF *Deepwater Horizon* oil spill-related claims processes.

This report is the third and final in a series of reports related to these objectives. In November 2010, we provided our preliminary assessment of the financial risks and the cost reimbursement and notification policies

---

[3]For any one oil pollution incident, the Fund may pay up to $1 billion. Fund expenditures for natural resource damage assessments and claims in connection with a single incident are limited to $500 million of that $1 billion.

[4]BP established the trust under Delaware law, which generally provides that the principal of the trust can be used only for the purposes stated in the trust agreement and that the terms of the agreement cannot be modified and are legally enforceable by the trustees.

and procedures associated with the *Deepwater Horizon* oil spill.[5] We expressed the view that Congress should consider changing the calculation of expenditures made against the Fund's $1 billion per incident expenditure cap to take into account reimbursements from responsible parties. We also made four recommendations to NPFC directed at helping NPFC establish and maintain effective cost reimbursement policies and procedures for the Fund and update NPFC's current policies to reflect current organization, structure, and management directives. (See appendix I for the specific recommendations and their status.) In April 2011, we provided updated information on the financial risks to the federal government associated with the Fund's cap on total, rather than net, expenditures, as well as claims submitted to and reviewed by NPFC and GCCF.[6] This final report provides an update on the issues and risks to the federal government, the results of our testing of NPFC's internal controls over the processes and payments for cost reimbursement and the claims process, and an overview of the federal government's oversight of BP and GCCF's claims processes.

As part of our analysis of financial risks to the federal government and the Fund, we identified and analyzed applicable laws and regulations to determine statutory and regulatory limitations on the liability of responsible parties that may pose financial risks to the Fund and federal government. As one of OPA's goals is to make the environment and public whole for injuries to natural resources resulting from an oil spill, we reviewed applicable guidance, regulations, and NPFC annual reports to gain an understanding of the Natural Resource Damage Assessment[7] process. These processes involve determining the type and amount of restoration needed to compensate the public for harm to natural resources as a result of an oil spill, and the length of time these assessments may take to complete. In addition, we reviewed publicly

---

[5]GAO, *Deepwater Horizon Oil Spill: Preliminary Assessment of Federal Financial Risks and Cost Reimbursement and Notification Policies and Procedures*, GAO-11-90R (Washington, D.C.: Nov. 12, 2010).

[6]GAO, *Deepwater Horizon Oil Spill: Update on Federal Financial Risks and Claims Processing*, GAO-11-397R (Washington, D.C.: Apr. 18, 2011).

[7]Natural resource damage assessments are conducted to evaluate the nature and extent of injuries resulting from an oil spill, and to determine restoration actions needed to bring injured natural resources and services back to what they were prior to the incident.

available quarterly financial information of responsible parties through June 2011 to gain an understanding of the extent to which these companies reported contingent liabilities.[8] To determine the amounts obligated and actual costs incurred in relation to the Fund's $1 billion per incident cap, we obtained and analyzed daily financial summary data NPFC uses to track costs for the *Deepwater Horizon* oil spill. We obtained invoices NPFC sent to the responsible parties to reimburse the Fund, analyzed the requests for reimbursements submitted by federal and state agencies, and compared the invoiced amounts to the amounts federal and state agencies had submitted for payment from the Fund.

To assess the extent to which NPFC's internal controls ensured that cost reimbursements were appropriate, we tested a statistical sample of payments made to federal and state agencies between April 2010 and April 2011 for *Deepwater Horizon* removal and response activities for compliance with NPFC's policies and procedures. In addition, while NPFC had not made any payments in response to claims from individuals and businesses submitted as of April 30, 2011, we tested a statistical sample of *Deepwater Horizon* final claim determinations—all denials or withdrawn by the claimant—that had been made by NPFC officials for compliance with NPFC's policies and procedures to implement OPA requirements. We also obtained information on NPFC's claims contingency planning for handling a potentially large number of claims related to the *Deepwater Horizon* oil spill. In order to update information about claims submitted and reviewed by NPFC and GCCF, we used available NPFC and GCCF claims data through May 31, 2011.

To provide an overview of the extent to which the federal government oversees the BP and the GCCF claims processes, we interviewed agency officials about oversight of BP's claims process. Specifically, we interviewed Department of Justice (Justice) officials who worked with BP to establish the GCCF and its claims processes, among other things. We also interviewed NPFC officials who monitor GCCF's actions to approve and deny claims from individuals and businesses. We interviewed Justice and Office of Management and Budget (OMB) officials about any plans to pursue payment from the responsible parties for federal government

---

[8]Contingent liabilities are potential liabilities that stem from an existing condition, situation, or set of circumstances involving uncertainty as to poss ble loss to an entity. The uncertainty will ultimately be resolved when one or more future events occur or fail to occur.

costs for the *Deepwater Horizon* oil spill that are not reimbursed through an intragovernmental agency agreement. Appendix II provides additional details on our scope and methodology.

We conducted this performance audit from July 2010 to October 2011, in accordance with generally accepted government auditing standards. Those standards require that we plan and perform the audit to obtain sufficient, appropriate evidence to provide a reasonable basis for our findings and conclusions based on our audit objectives. We believe that the evidence obtained provides a reasonable basis for our findings and conclusions based on our audit objectives.

Background

Legal Framework Establishing Responsibilities to Pay Oil Spill Costs and Claims

The legal framework for addressing and paying for maritime oil spills is identified in OPA, which was enacted after the 1989 *Exxon Valdez* spill. OPA places the primary burden of liability and the costs of oil spills on the owner and operator of the vessel or on shore facility and the lessee or permittee of the area in which an offshore facility is located. This "polluter pays" framework requires that the responsible party or parties assume the burden of spill response, natural resource restoration, and compensation to those damaged by the spill, up to a specified limit of liability. In general, the level of potential exposure under OPA depends on the kind of vessel or facility from which a spill originates and is limited in amount unless the oil discharge is the result of gross negligence or willful misconduct, or a violation of federal operation, safety, and construction regulations, in which case liability under OPA is unlimited.[9] For oil spills from an offshore

---

[9]Under OPA, a responsible party can also assert a defense to liability if the oil spill was caused solely by, among other things, an "act of God," an "act of war," the acts or omissions of an independent third party (provided certain conditions are satisfied), or any combination of these. 33 U.S.C. 2703. NPFC guidance acknowledges that terrorism or other criminal acts may present a defense to liability under OPA. NPFC, *NPFC User Reference Guide (eURG)*, Appendix B, *Federal On-Scene Coordinator Funding Information for Oil Spills and Hazardous Materials Releases* (Washington, D.C.: April 2003), available at http://uscg.mil/npfc/URG/default.asp.

facility, such as the *Deepwater Horizon*, liability is limited to all removal—or cleanup—costs plus $75 million.[10]

Under OPA, before any vessel larger than 300 gross tons can operate in U.S. waters, the owner/operator must obtain a Certificate of Financial Responsibility (COFR) from NPFC. This COFR demonstrates that the owner/operator has provided evidence of financial responsibility to pay for removal costs and damages up to the liability limits required by OPA. These OPA requirements for demonstrating financial responsibility apply only to the statutory maximum amount of potential liability under OPA, although states may impose additional liabilities and requirements related to oil spills in state waters.[11]

OPA requires that, subject to certain exceptions, such as removal cost claims by states, all nonfederal claims for OPA-compensable removal or damages be submitted first to the responsible party or the responsible party's guarantor. If the responsible party denies a claim or does not settle it within 90 days, a claimant may present the claim to the federal government to be considered for payment.[12] To pay specified claims above a responsible party's liability limit, as well as to pay claims when a responsible party does not pay or cannot be identified, OPA authorizes use of the Fund subject to limitations on the amount and types of costs. For example, under OPA, the authorized limit on Fund expenditures for a single spill is currently set at $1 billion (without consideration of whether the Fund was reimbursed for any expenditures). In addition to paying claims, the Fund is used to reimburse government agencies for certain eligible costs they incur. Further, within the $1 billion cap, the costs for conducting a natural resource damage assessment and claims paid in connection with any single incident shall not exceed $500 million. OPA provides that the President designate the federal officials and that the governors designate the state and local officials who act on behalf of the

---

[10]Removal costs are incurred by the federal government or any other entity taking approved action to contain and clean up the spill.

[11]Users of offshore facilities on outer continental shelf lands have similar requirements to those covering vessels. Under OPA, they must submit evidence of an Oil Spill Financial Responsibility for an offshore facility (that generally is capable of discharging more than 1,000 barrels of oil) to the Department of Interior (DOI) and receive approval. DOI's regulations for the process are set out in 30 C.F.R. part 253.

[12]See appendix III for NPFC's individual and business claims process.

public as trustees for natural resources.[13] OPA regulations provide that the trustees may recover costs for natural resource damage assessment and restoration.[14] The Fund may not be used for certain types of personal injuries or damages that may arise related to an oil spill incident, such as financial losses associated with oil company investments by members of the public. Recovery for such damages and injuries may be governed by other federal statutes, common law, or various state laws.

Federal agencies are authorized to use the Fund to cover their oil removal costs from the affected areas to the extent the Fund has funds available within the $1 billion cap.[15] The federal government is entitled to reimbursement from responsible parties for such costs.

The Coast Guard's NPFC administers uses of the Fund to reimburse government agencies for their removal and cleanup costs;[16] adjudicating individual and business claims submitted to the Fund for payment; and pursuing reimbursement from the responsible party for costs and claims paid by the Fund. NPFC bills the responsible parties directly, including BP in this case, for costs government agencies have incurred, and all payments received from responsible parties are deposited into the Fund.

OPA defines the costs for which responsible parties are liable and for which the Fund is made available for compensation in the event that the responsible party does not pay, cannot pay, or is not identified. As described in greater detail in appendix V, "OPA compensable" costs include two main types:

- Removal Costs: Removal costs are incurred by the federal government or any other entity taking approved action to respond to, contain, and clean up the spill. For example, removal costs include cleaning up adjoining shoreline affected by the oil spill and the equipment used in the response—skimmers to pull oil from the water,

---

[13]33 U.S.C. 2706.

[14]15 C.F.R. 990.41; 15 C.F.R. 990.65.

[15]Affected areas may include both water and land resources, such as waterways or beaches.

[16]Appendix IV discusses NPFC's cost reimbursement process.

booms to contain the oil, planes for aerial observation—as well as salaries, travel, and lodging costs for responders.

- Damages: OPA-compensable damages cover a wide range of both actual and potential adverse impacts from an oil spill. For example, damages from an oil spill include the loss of profits to the owner of a commercial charter boat if the boat was trapped in port because the Coast Guard closed the waterway in order to remove the oil, or personal property damage to the owner of a recreational boat or waterfront property that was oiled by the spill, for which a claim may be made first to the responsible party, if possible, or to the Fund.

In addition to OPA-compensable costs, the federal government can also incur other non OPA-compensable costs associated with oil spills. For example, the federal government had various non-OPA-compensable costs for the *Deepwater Horizon* oil spill, such as Department of Homeland Security (DHS) costs associated with providing additional staff to NPFC for receiving and processing claims.[17]

Four Operational Response Phases for Oil Removal

The *National Oil and Hazardous Substances Pollution Contingency Plan*, more commonly called the National Contingency Plan is the federal government's blueprint for responding to oil spill and hazardous substance releases. The National Contingency Plan provides the organizational structure and procedures for preparing for and responding to discharges of oil and releases of hazardous substances, pollutants, and contaminants.[18] The plan outlines approved procedures and removal activities when responding to an oil spill and identifies the following four phases of response operations for oil discharges:

1. Discovery and Notification include activities conducted to discover oil spills or to notify appropriate authorities of oil spills.
2. Preliminary Assessment and Initiation of Action include activities conducted to assess the magnitude and severity of the spill and to assess the feasibility of removal and plan appropriate actions. These activities are necessary whether or not the responsible party is taking action.

---

[17]If a claim were paid by the Fund, the Fund could recover administrative costs attributable to the claim under 33 U.S.C. 2715.

[18]40 C.F.R. Part 300.

3. Containment, Countermeasures, Cleanup, and Disposal include oil spill cleanup activities such as hiring contractors and transporting and staging required supplies and needed equipment.
4. Documentation and Cost Recovery include the activities necessary to support cost recovery and record uses of the Fund.

Three of the four phases for oil removal remain under way for the *Deepwater Horizon* incident, and the operational response is likely to continue for years. The first phase, discovery and notification, is substantially complete. Subject to certain thresholds, the costs incurred in phases two, three, and four are eligible to be paid from the Fund.

The Fund's Financial Resources to Pay Oil Spill Costs and Claims

The Fund's primary revenue source is an 8 cent per barrel tax on petroleum products either produced in the United States or imported from other countries. Other revenue sources include recoveries from responsible parties for costs of removal and damages, fines and penalties paid pursuant to various statutes, and interest earned on the Fund's U.S. Treasury investments. In fiscal year 2009, the barrel tax was 92 percent of the Fund's revenue. As shown in figure 1, the Fund's balance has varied over the years. The barrel tax expired in December 1994 and was reinstituted at 5 cents per barrel in April 2006 as mandated by the Energy Policy Act of 2005. The Energy Improvement and Extension Act of 2008 increased the tax to 8 cents per barrel and provides that the Fund's barrel tax shall expire after December 31, 2017.[19]

---

[19]Pub. L. No. 110-343, § 405, 122 Stat. 3765, 3860 (Oct. 3, 2008).

Figure 1: Oil Spill Liability Trust Fund Balance, September 1993–May 2011 (Unaudited)

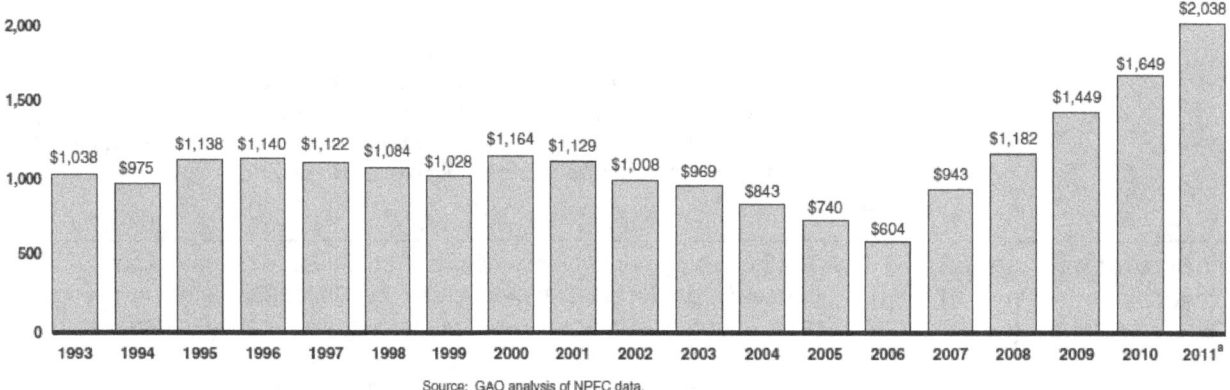

Source: GAO analysis of NPFC data.

[a]Fund balance as of May 31, 2011 (unaudited).

In fiscal year 2011, the increase to the Fund is primarily attributable to reimbursements received from responsible parties for the Coast Guard's costs incurred in response to the *Deepwater Horizon* incident. Specifically, as of May 31, 2011, the Coast Guard has billed and received from responsible parties, $315.3 million for Coast Guard recoverable, or indirect costs, such as personnel and equipment. According to the agency, the Coast Guard has historically viewed its OPA recoverable costs as activities normally funded through the agency's operating expense appropriation, and thus it has not sought reimbursement for these costs from the Fund.

As shown in figure 2, the Fund has been administratively divided into two major components—the Emergency Fund and the Principal Fund— administered by the Coast Guard's NPFC. The Emergency Fund authorizes the President to make available $50 million each year to cover immediate expenses associated with mitigating the threat of an oil spill, costs of oil spill containment, countermeasures, and cleanup and disposal activities, as well as paying for other costs to initiate natural resource damage assessments. Amounts made available remain available until expended. For the *Deepwater Horizon* oil spill, the Coast Guard's Federal On-Scene Coordinator[20] used the Emergency Fund to pay for oil spill removal activities (i.e., the equipment used in removal activities and for the proper disposal of recovered oil and oil debris), and the Federal Natural Resource Damage Trustees[21] also entered into reimbursable agreements with NPFC with respect to funding for activities to initiate natural resource damage assessments. To the extent that available amounts are inadequate for an emergency (as was the case in the *Deepwater Horizon* oil spill), the Maritime Transportation Security Act of 2002 granted authority for the Coast Guard to advance up to $100 million to pay for oil spill removal activities, and that amount was advanced from the Principal Fund to the Emergency Fund.[22]

---

[20]The Federal On-Scene Coordinator has responsibility for overseeing oil spill response efforts and determining that efforts were conducted in accordance with the National Contingency Plan. To pay government agencies' oil spill removal costs, the Federal On-Scene Coordinator issues authorizations to quickly obtain services and assistance from government agencies, verifies that the services or goods were received and consistent with the National Contingency Plan, certifies the supporting documentation, and sends the cost documentation to NPFC, which authorizes the Coast Guard's Finance Center to pay the government agencies.

[21]OPA provides for the designation of federal, state, and if designated by the Governor of the state, local officials, to act on behalf of the public as trustees for natural resources. In addition, OPA provides for designations of Indian tr be and foreign officials to act as trustees for natural resources on behalf of, respectively, the tribe or its members and the foreign government.

[22]Pub. L. No. 107-295, § 323, 116 Stat. 2064, 2104 (Nov. 25, 2002).

Figure 2: Oil Spill Liability Trust Fund Components

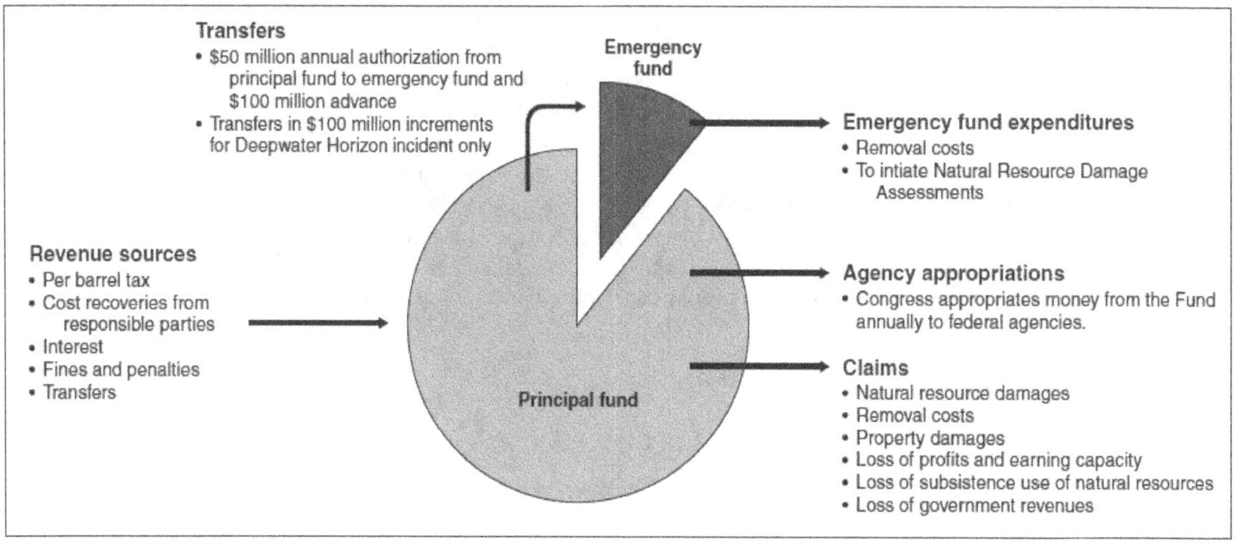

Transfers
- $50 million annual authorization from principal fund to emergency fund and $100 million advance
- Transfers in $100 million increments for Deepwater Horizon incident only

Emergency fund

Emergency fund expenditures
- Removal costs
- To intiate Natural Resource Damage Assessments

Revenue sources
- Per barrel tax
- Cost recoveries from responsible parties
- Interest
- Fines and penalties
- Transfers

Principal fund

Agency appropriations
- Congress appropriates money from the Fund annually to federal agencies.

Claims
- Natural resource damages
- Removal costs
- Property damages
- Loss of profits and earning capacity
- Loss of subsistence use of natural resources
- Loss of government revenues

Sources: NPFC and DHS USCG Report on implementation of the Oil Pollution Act of 1990.

In June 2010, Congress amended OPA to authorize emergency advances for the *Deepwater Horizon* oil spill in increments of up to $100 million for each cash advance, but the total amount of all advances may not exceed the $1 billion per incident cap.[23] In contrast to the Emergency Fund, the Principal Fund is to be used to provide funds for natural resource damage claims,[24] loss of profits and earning capacity claims, and loss of government revenues. The Principal Fund also provides for certain agency appropriations including the Coast Guard, Environmental Protection Agency (EPA), and the Department of the Interior (DOI)—each of which receives an annual appropriation from the Fund through the Principal Fund to cover administrative, operational, personnel, and enforcement costs.

[23]Pub. L. No. 111-191 § 1, 124 Stat. 1278 (June 15, 2010).

[24]Natural resource damage claims are claims for natural resource damages arising out of oil spills and include costs to restore, rehabilitate, replace, or acquire the equivalent of the injured resource, any interim lost use or diminution in value of the injured resource pending restoration, and the reasonable cost of assessing those damages.

Consistent with its Fund management responsibilities, in response to the *Deepwater Horizon* oil spill, NPFC is responsible for billing the responsible parties, including BP, directly for costs that government agencies have incurred. The payments NPFC receives from BP are to be deposited into the Fund and NPFC reimburses agencies for their removal costs.

Funds are to be disbursed from the Fund to government agencies using two vehicles—Pollution Removal Funding Authorizations (PRFA) and Military Interdepartmental Purchase Requests (MIPR). The PRFA commits the Fund to reimburse costs incurred for agreed-upon pollution response activities undertaken by a federal agency assisting the Federal On-Scene Coordinator. The terms of a PRFA include relevant (1) personnel salary costs, (2) travel and per diem expenses, (3) charges for the use of agency-owned equipment or facilities, and (4) expenses for contractor or vendor-supplied goods or services obtained by the agency for removal assistance. Similarly, the Federal On-Scene Coordinator may issue a MIPR for agreed-upon activities of the Department of Defense (DOD) or its related components and for some other agencies' activities. In contrast to PRFAs, MIPRs generally commit the Fund to disburse funds for oil spill response activities prior to conducting the activity and incurring the related costs. However, for the *Deepwater Horizon* oil spill, both NPFC and DOD established procedures for submitting documentation on a regular basis for MIPRs authorized in response to this spill of national significance.

BP's Claims Process for Individuals and Businesses

The Coast Guard, without in any way relieving the other responsible parties it identified of liability, approved BP's advertisement of its claims process.[25] In response to economic harm caused by the *Deepwater Horizon* oil spill and to fulfill its obligations as a responsible party, BP established a claims process and multiple claims centers throughout the Gulf states. On May 3, 2010, BP began paying emergency compensation to individuals and businesses. BP stated that emergency payments would continue as long as individuals and businesses could show they were unable to earn a living because of injury to natural resources caused by

---

[25]On May 11, 2010, NPFC notified BP and Transocean Holdings Incorporated that BP's advertisement of its claims process was sufficient, and Transocean should not advertise and should coordinate claims processing with BP. According to NPFC officials, they wanted to avoid public confusion and have only one responsible party advertise for claims.

the oil spill. According to BP, it would base emergency payments on 1 month of income and would be adjusted with additional documentation.[26] BP has been working to ensure that the other *Deepwater Horizon* oil spill responsible parties contribute to the response. On May 20, 2011, BP announced that it had reached an agreement with MOEX Offshore 2007 LLC and its affiliates to settle all claims between the companies related to the *Deepwater Horizon* oil spill, which included MOEX paying $1.065 billion to BP. Additionally, on October 17, 2011, BP announced that it had reached an agreement with Anadarko Petroleum Company to settle all claims between the companies related to the Deepwater Horizon oil spill, which included Anadarko paying $4 billion to BP.

On June 16, 2010, President Obama announced that BP had agreed to set aside $20 billion to pay certain economic damage claims caused by the oil spill.[27] On August 6, 2010, BP established an irrevocable Trust and committed to fund it on a quarterly basis over 3-1/2 years to reach the $20 billion total (as shown in fig. 3). The Trust is to pay some OPA-compensable claims as well as some other claims for personal injuries that are not OPA-compensable, but for which BP would be liable under other law.[28]

---

[26]*Legal Liability Issues Surrounding the Gulf Coast Oil Disaster:* Hearing Before the H. Comm. on the Judiciary, 111th Cong. 85-92 (2010) (statement of Darryl Willis, Vice President, Resources, BP America).

[27]Under terms of the Trust, BP may be called upon to pay non-economic damages as a result of litigation or other settlements.

[28]For example, 46 U.S.C. § 30104, (commonly known as the Jones Act),establishes liability for injury or death of seamen incurred in the course of their employment. For additional information regarding the oil spill legal framework, see enclosure III in our November 2010 product (GAO-11-90R).

Figure 3: The Trust's $20 Billion Funding Time Frame

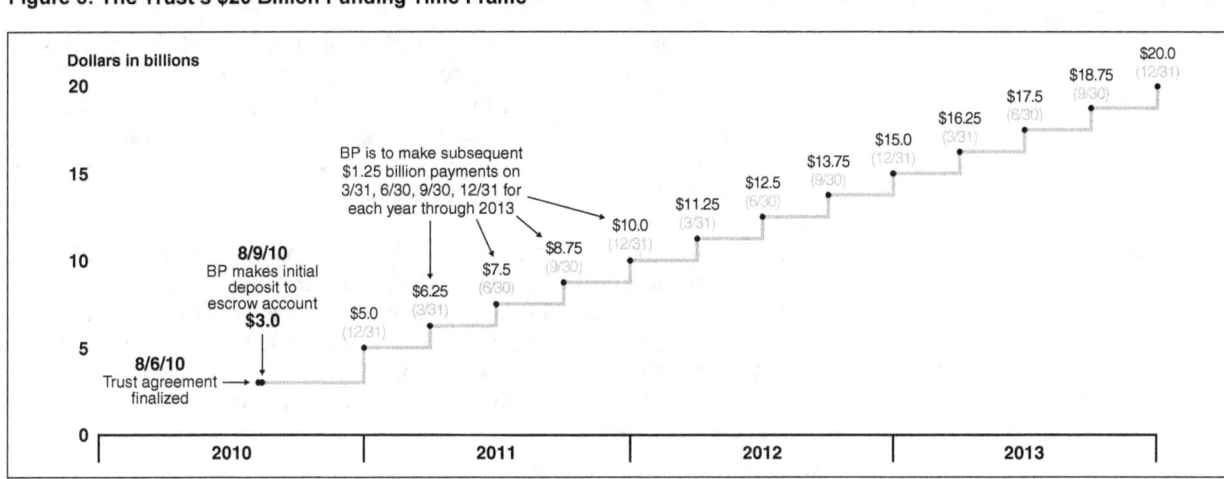

Source: GAO analysis of an August 9, 2010 BP press release on the funding of the $20 billion account.

On August 23, 2010, the GCCF took over the administration of claims process and the centers BP had established.[29] Since it began operating, the GCCF has offered the following kinds of payments:

- Emergency Advance Payments: Payments available to individuals and businesses that were experiencing financial hardship resulting from damages incurred from the *Deepwater Horizon* oil spill. GCCF considered claims on emergency payments that were submitted by November 23, 2010.
- Quick Payment Final Claim: On December 13, 2010, BP announced that individuals and businesses that had received emergency payments from the GCCF were eligible for a quick payment final claim, which offers a fixed amount of $5,000 for individuals and $25,000 for businesses. Acceptance of such a claim would resolve all claims by that claimant against BP including past and future alleged damages. The GCCF Protocols for Interim and Final Claims provides

---

[29]On September 1, 2011, the GCCF closed 7 of the claims centers due to reduced activity and need for the centers.

GAO-12-86 *Deepwater Horizon* Oil Spill

that final claims can be submitted to the GCCF through August 23, 2013.[30]

- Final Payment: Those who do not choose or are not eligible for the quick payment may submit a full review final payment claim for all documented losses and damages. Acceptance of a final claim would resolve all claims by that claimant against BP including past and future alleged damages. Under GCCF procedures, claimants will have until August 23, 2013, to estimate damages and submit claims for final payment.
- Interim Payments: The alternative to a final payment is to make an interim payment claim for past damages that have not been compensated. Individuals and businesses receiving interim payments are not required to sign a release of liability and may file a final claim at a later date. The GCCF Protocols for Interim and Final Claims provides that interim claims can be submitted to the GCCF through August 23, 2013.

As of May 31 2011, GCCF has paid $4.2 billion for individual and business claims as shown in table 1. While the GCCF is scheduled to stop receiving claims on August 23, 2013, BP's obligation, as a responsible party under OPA, to receive claims will continue after the GCCF closes.

Table 1: Claims Paid by GCCF as of May 31, 2011 (Unaudited)

Dollars in millions

Type	Number of claims paid	Amount
Emergency Advanced Payments	169,142	$2,582.6
Interim Payments	12,977	147.8
Quick Pay (Final)[a]	114,320	1,105.4
Full Review (Final)[a]	25,102	390.5
Total[b]	321,541	$4,226.3

Source: GAO analysis of GCCF data.

[a]Both Quick Pay and Full Review require he claimants to sign a release waiving any rights they may have against responsible parties to file or participate in legal action or to submit any claim to NPFC for payment.

[b]As described in our November 2010 report, claims approved by GCCF are paid from a Trust established and funded (up to $20 billion) by BP. Prior to the establishment of GCCF, BP had received and directly paid claims from individuals and businesses totaling $396.0 million.

[30]GCCF, *Gulf Coast Claims Facility Protocol for Interim and Final Claims* (Nov. 22, 2010).

Although the Total Federal Financial Risk Has Not Been Determined, Actions Are Needed to Reduce Known Risks

Both the individual circumstances of the *Deepwater Horizon* incident, as well as the overall framework of how the federal government responds to oil spills, present a mix of financial risks to the Fund and the federal government. The extent of financial risks to the federal government from the *Deepwater Horizon* is closely tied to BP and the other responsible parties and guarantors. Because the federal government's Fund would pay if the responsible party (BP through its Trust, for example) did not, and given the expectation for numerous expenses to be paid from the Trust and the fact that the full amount of damages may not be fully determined for some time, the extent of any long-term financial risks for the federal government as a result of this spill is not clear. Federal agency cleanup and restoration activities are underway and agencies continue to incur costs and submit them for reimbursement. As a result, it is possible that expenditures from the Fund for Federal removal costs and claims will reach the $1 billion cap, as the cap balance was over $626 million on May 31, 2011.[31] When the cap balance reaches the total expenditure cap of $1 billion, no further payments to reimburse agencies' costs (or to pay individual or business claims if not paid by the responsible parties) can be made from the Fund, so federal agencies would no longer be able to obtain reimbursement for their costs. Finally, the federal government's longer-term ability to provide financial support in response to future oil spills is also at risk because the Fund's primary source of revenue, a tax on petroleum products, is scheduled to expire in 2017.

---

[31]The current cap balance is calculated by NPFC and consists of the actual expenditures from the Fund and amounts obligated by NPFC but have yet to be expended from the Fund.

BP Has Committed to Paying *Deepwater Horizon* Expenses, but the Extent of the Federal Government's Financial Exposure Remains Unknown

BP has committed to set aside $20 billion to cover potential *Deepwater Horizon* oil spill expenses[32]—and has stated its intent to pay expenses over the $20 billion if needed. BP's track record for reimbursing federal agencies for their expenses to this point has been favorable. For example, as of May 31, 2011, NPFC had sent 11 invoices to all of the responsible parties covering federal and state OPA-compensable costs totaling $711 million and BP paid all 11 invoices.[33] However, until the total expenses of the *Deepwater Horizon* oil spill have been fully determined and those amounts have then been paid by and reimbursed to the federal government, the extent of any federal government financial exposure remains unknown.[34] The financial responsibility for the spill will ultimately be determined through a lengthy and complex process involving the application of different laws and regulations, and depends upon a continuation of the ability of the responsible parties to pay expenses associated with the *Deepwater Horizon* oil spill.[35]

Although BP has established a $20 billion Trust to pay claims from individuals and businesses harmed by the spill, a number of uncertainties regarding the Trust's uses may impact its ability to adequately reimburse claimants, increasing the risk that the federal government will ultimately be responsible for paying the remaining claims. Although all uncertainties—and the associated expenses—may not be known for many years, some uncertainties that are known relate to the following issues.

- The federal government has begun an extensive natural resource damage assessment process, but the associated costs have yet to be determined. In order to start the process, in May 2010, BP agreed to provide $10 million to DOI and $10 million to the National Oceanic

---

[32]BP has established collateral for the remaining portion of the $20 billion yet to be funded.

[33]NPFC has billed the responsible parties based on a combination of Coast Guard actual costs and a percentage of the amount NPFC has obligated for agencies through PRFAs and MIPRs.

[34]The United States has not encountered a spill comparable to the *Deepwater Horizon* oil spill since the 1989 *Exxon Valdez* spill, which reported that its natural resource damages were at least $1 billion (within the $1 billion cap the Fund has a $500 million statutory limit on natural resource damage assessments and claims). The responsible parties can pay natural resource damage assessment costs directly to the relevant federal agencies.

[35]Enclosure III of our November 2010 report (GAO-11-90R) discusses the legal framework of oil spills.

and Atmospheric Administration (NOAA) in the Department of Commerce. Also, in April 2011, BP committed up to $1 billion from the Trust to projects to help restore damaged natural resources in the Gulf of Mexico, such as the rebuilding of costal marshes, replenishment of damaged beaches, conservation of sensitive areas for ocean habitat for injured wildlife, and restoration of barrier islands and wetlands that provide natural protection from storms. The natural resource damage assessment and restoration process will take years to complete, so the full costs for which BP and the other responsible parties are liable have yet to be determined. The National Commission on BP Deepwater Horizon Oil Spill and Offshore Drilling report estimates that fully restoring the Gulf will take $15 billion to $20 billion and over 30 years.[36] If the responsible parties are unable or unwilling to pay, then the agencies' costs for the natural resource damages, including the costs to assess and restore, rehabilitate, replace, or acquire equivalent natural resources, would need to be reimbursed from the Fund (provided that funds were still available, given the $1 billion per incident cap).

- The responsible parties also are likely to face fines and penalties which have yet to be determined and which will be levied by federal and state governments. In particular, under the Clean Water Act, liable parties face substantial administrative and civil penalties that may be imposed by EPA or DHS.[37] According to the BP Oil Spill Commission Report, the maximum Clean Water Act civil penalties could range from $4.5 billion to $21 billion.

- BP and the other responsible parties face over 500 lawsuits from the federal government, states, investors, employees, businesses, and individuals. The extent to which these lawsuits will impact the responsible parties financially is uncertain at this time since they will take years to litigate. BP has stated that it may use the Trust to pay lawsuit settlements as well as for paying claims and for natural resource damages.

- Justice is continuing to evaluate federal government costs incurred related to the *Deepwater Horizon* oil spill that are not OPA-

---

[36]The National Commission on BP Deepwater Horizon Oil Spill and Offshore Drilling was established through Exec. Order No. 13,543 (May 21, 2010) to examine the relevant facts and circumstances concerning the root causes of the *Deepwater Horizon* explosion and developed options to guard against, and mitigate the impact of, any oil spills associated with offshore drilling in the future. The Commission's respons bilities include recommending improvements to federal laws, regulations, and industry practices.

[37]33 U.S.C. 1321(b) (6) and (7).

compensable. On May 13, 2011, Justice sent the responsible parties an invoice requesting reimbursement to the federal government for $81.6 million (for agencies' costs incurred through December 2010).

Although BP has stated that it will pay expenses over the $20 billion, if necessary, it is uncertain how this would be accomplished over time, thus posing an element of risk to the federal government. In addition, although MOEX and its affiliates have settled with BP by paying $1.065 billion and Anadarko settled with BP which included a payment of $4 billion, other responsible parties have not reached a settlement. If BP becomes unable to pay future cleanup costs, individual and business claims, and natural resource restoration costs, the federal government may need to consider paying costs and then pursuing reimbursement from the other responsible parties.

Reaching the Fund's $1 Billion Cap Could Result in Federal Agencies Needing Additional Funding for Oil Spill Response Costs

NPFC's *Deepwater Horizon* oil spill amounts counted towards this cap was $626.1 million as of May 31, 2011, and is thereby approaching the $1 billion per-incident cap mandated by OPA. The $626.1 million consists of $128.0 million incurred by the Coast Guard and $498.1 million incurred by other agencies. Once expenditures from the Fund reach the cap, NPFC will be statutorily barred from reimbursing federal agencies for response and restoration work, or paying individuals and businesses to settle claims. Consequently, if federal agencies did not receive dedicated appropriations for oil spill costs, the federal agencies would be faced with reallocating their appropriated funding to cover oil spill costs, or seeking additional funding from Congress. In November 2010, we suggested that Congress may want to consider setting a Fund cap associated with an incident, based upon net expenditures (expenditures less reimbursements).[38]

As of May 31, 2011, government agencies continue to submit documentation of their *Deepwater Horizon* oil spill recovery costs for reimbursement from the Fund. (App. VII provides information about government agencies' authorized response costs and amounts reimbursed.) Further, although as of May 31, 2011 all individual and business claims reviewed by NPFC have been denied, claims continue to

---

[38]GAO-11-90R.

be submitted.[39] According to NPFC officials, individuals and businesses will continue to submit claims associated with the *Deepwater Horizon* oil spill for several years. In addition, the natural resources restoration process is beginning and these associated costs will accumulate over many years.

Uncertainties Regarding Future Funding Availability

Uncertainties exist regarding the primary revenue source of the Fund, which is set to expire in 2017, and the potential for future oil spills. If the Fund's primary source of revenue expires, this could affect future oil spill response and may increase risk to the federal government. Also, although the *Deepwater Horizon* oil spill was the largest oil spill disaster in U.S. history, annually over 500 spills of varying size and response occur.

- The per barrel tax revenue. A provision of The Energy Improvement and Extension Act of 2008 mandates that the Fund's primary source of revenue, a per barrel tax, is set to expire on December 31, 2017.[40] Therefore, even with substantial amounts reimbursed by BP, the Fund balance would likely decrease as a result of the expiration of its primary source of funding and the expectation of future *Deepwater Horizon* costs. This could raise the risk that the Fund would not be adequately equipped to deal with future spills, particularly one of this magnitude, and it will be important for Congress to determine a funding mechanism for the Fund going forward. The two other sources of revenue are cost recoveries from responsible parties and interest on the Fund principal from U.S. Treasury investments.[41] As we reported in September 2007,[42] the balance of the Fund generally declined from 1995 to 2006 mostly because the per barrel tax expired

---

[39]As of May 31, 2011, all 570 individual and business claims finalized by NPFC have been denied for reasons such as failure to demonstrate that damages were the result of the spill and lack of documentation.

[40]Pub. L. No. 110-343, div. B, tit. IV § 405(b), 122 Stat. 3765, 3861 (Oct. 3, 2008).

[41]In fiscal year 2010, the Fund received $475.9 million from the per barrel tax, $518.4 million from payments related to *Deepwater Horizon,* and $18.7 million from interest on investments.

[42]GAO, *Maritime Transportation: Major Oil Spills Occur Infrequently, but Risks to the Federal Oil Spill Fund Remain,* GAO-07-1085 (Washington D.C.: Sept. 7, 2007).

in December 1994 and revenue was not collected from January 1995 to March 2006.[43]

- The potential need to fund the response to future spills poses risks. The possibility of needing to respond to another spill of national significance increases the risk to the Fund and the federal government. In fiscal year 2011 alone, the Fund has already paid for 267 oil spills through May 31, 2011. According to NPFC officials, on an annual basis, approximately 500 spills with varying costs and magnitude occur. In 2007, we reported that since 1990 approximately 51 spills amounting to over $1 million have occurred, and that responsible parties and the Fund have spent between $860 million and $1.1 billion for oil spill removal costs and compensation for damages.[44] Responsible parties paid between 72 and 78 percent of these expenses, while the Fund paid the remainder. As of May 31, 2011, the Fund's balance was approximately $2.0 billion. The federal government would need to consider using other sources of funds particularly if another spill of national significance occurs and if the responsible party(ies) are unable or unwilling to pay.

The Coast Guard Has Effective Claims Processing and Cost Reimbursement Controls, However Could Benefit by Documenting Changes Made in Claims Practices

Our testing of the Coast Guard's controls over *Deepwater Horizon* claims processed as of April 30, 2011, and cost reimbursements processed as of April 20, 2011, showed that adjudicated claims processed and costs reimbursed were consistent with its procedures. The Coast Guard's operating practices in these areas have changed to reflect the largely unprecedented size and evolving scope of the *Deepwater Horizon* incident. It has updated its cost reimbursement procedures to incorporate lessons learned from the initial response to this spill and although it has not yet updated its procedures for processing claims from spills of national significance to reflect lessons learned from its experiences processing *Deepwater Horizon* claims, it has plans to do so.

---

[43]The tax expired in December 1994 and was reinstated by the Energy Policy Act of 2005 beginning April 2006.

[44]GAO-07-1085.

Tests Show Coast Guard's NPFC Has Established Effective Controls for Processing *Deepwater Horizon* Claims and Cost Reimbursements

We found that internal controls related to the documentation, review, and adjudication of individual and business claims submitted following the *Deepwater Horizon* oil spill were operating in accordance with established policies and procedures. During the period September 1, 2010, through May 31, 2011, NPFC received 901 *Deepwater Horizon* claims totaling $238 million. Of these claims, NPFC has finalized 570, all of which resulted in a denial or a withdrawal by the claimant.

Our testing of a statistical sample of 60 out of the 432 *Deepwater Horizon* finalized claims through April 30, 2011 found that NPFC had followed its policies and procedures.[45] Specifically, all claims

- were submitted in writing, for a sum certain amount, and included the required claimant information (i.e., address, nature and extent of the impact of the incident, etc.);
- complied with OPA's order of presentment (which requires that all claims for removal costs or damages must be presented first to the responsible party for payment), and verified that claimants had filed with the responsible party first before submitting their claim to NPFC;
- included evidence submitted by the claimant, or if needed, NPFC sent a letter to the claimant requesting additional support;
- were adjudicated within the time provided by regulation;[46]
- underwent legal review and were submitted within the required time frame, if reconsideration was requested;[47] and
- when denied, were appropriately transmitted by sending a denial letter to the claimant along with a Claim Summary/Determination Form explaining the basis for denial.

However, because all finalized claims resulted in denials or withdrawals, our testing could not assess the effectiveness of NPFC's controls over payments to individuals and business claimants.

---

[45]As of May 31, 2011, NPFC had finalized 570 claims. Our sample for claims testing was selected from the 432 claims finalized as of April 30, 2011.

[46]According to 33 C.F.R. 136.115(c), if NPFC fails to make final disposition of a claim within 6 months after it is filed, at the option of the claimant any time thereafter, be deemed a final denial of the claim.

[47]A request for reconsideration must be received by NPFC within 60 calendar days after the date the denial was mailed to the claimant or within 30 days after receipt of the denial by the claimant, whichever is earlier. 33 C.F.R. 136.115(d).

Our statistical testing of 57 of 954 *Deepwater Horizon* cost reimbursements for government oil spill response activities from the Fund between April 20, 2010, and April 20, 2011, found that in all cases NPFC had followed established policies and procedures. Specifically, NPFC

- accepted only cost reimbursement packages from government agencies with a signed PRFA or MIPR agreement in place for *Deepwater Horizon* response costs;
- determined that the Federal On-Scene Coordinator certified that all services or goods were received;
- ensured that supporting cost documentation submitted for reimbursement complied with the PRFA statement of work or MIPR agreement;
- wrote a letter to FINCEN[48] authorizing payment (signed by an NPFC Case Officer for the amount disbursed from the Fund under the appropriate PRFA or MIPR); and
- obtained supporting documentation from the government agency requesting reimbursement.

NPFC Updated Its Cost Reimbursement Procedures to Reflect Lessons Learned for *Deepwater Horizon*, and Plans to Similarly Update Its Claims Procedures

NPFC has strengthened its cost reimbursement guidance to reflect lessons learned from experiences during the initial *Deepwater Horizon* oil spill response, and officials told us they planned to take similar steps to update its claims processing guidance. Updating NPFC's claims procedures to fully reflect *Deepwater Horizon* lessons learned will be critical should another spill of national significance occur.

On April 14, 2011, NPFC issued an appendix for its cost reimbursement procedures manual modifying the procedures the agency is to follow for spills of national significance. This appendix is based on the lessons learned from addressing the unprecedented challenges posed by the *Deepwater Horizon* oil spill.[49] It provides guidance, for example, targeting some of the issues that arose related to the management of finances, including cost documentation requirements for MIPRs with DOD. Specifically, the modified procedures provide that MIPRs will be

---

[48]The Coast Guard's Finance Center (FINCEN) is located in Chesapeake, Va. and serves as the data center for finance and procurement, central bill paying and financial accounting center for the Coast Guard.

[49]U.S. Coast Guard, NPFC, *Case Management Division Standard Operating Procedures, CM SOP Appendix,* NPFCINST M16451.23, April 2011.

reimbursed after the cost documentation is reviewed and work completion verified.

NPFC officials told us that its current claims processing practices have also evolved since April 2010 to reflect lessons learned from the *Deepwater Horizon* oil spill. Over the past 10 years, NPFC typically received, on average, fewer than 300 claims each year. However, in light of the dramatic increase in the number of *Deepwater Horizon* oil spill claims received, NPFC refined its practices to augment its claims processing capacity. These practices included using contractors, Coast Guard reservists and, as needed, reassigning other NPFC staff. NPFC's *Standard Operating Procedures of the Claims Adjudication Division*, which have not been updated since April 2004, do not yet include specific procedures required for processing claims for a spill of national significance.[50] In particular, the procedures do not include modified practices to respond to the dramatic increase in claims filed as a result of the *Deepwater Horizon* incident. For the *Deepwater Horizon* oil spill, NPFC adopted practices involving newly developed performance indicators, past experience and continuous updates on current GCCF statistics as tools to identify the timing and extent of additional resources needed to augment its claims processing capabilities. GAO's *Standards of Internal Control in the Federal Government*[51] provide that internal control should provide for specific activities needed to help ensure management's directives are carried out.

NPFC has an opportunity to help ensure that expertise and effective practices are not lost by incorporating the lessons learned from the *Deepwater Horizon* incident in its guidance. Clearly documenting the policies and procedures used for the *Deepwater Horizon* incident would position NPFC for more effectively processing claims from any future spills of national significance by incorporating guidance, for example, on the use of performance indicators and statistics to address the size and timing of claim submissions. NPFC officials told us they are in the process of drafting an appendix for claims for spills of national significance for its

---

[50]U.S. Coast Guard, NPFC, *Standard Operating Procedures of the Claims Adjudication Division*, NPFCINST M16451.21 (April 2004).

[51]GAO, *Standards for Internal Control in the Federal Government*, GAO/AIMD-00-21.3.1 (Washington, D.C.: November 1999).

individual and business claims procedures manual to document such procedures.

Federal Agencies' Oversight Efforts Include Monitoring GCCF's Claims Process and Participating in Natural Resource Assessments

The federal government has used a variety of approaches to oversee BP's and GCCF's cost reimbursement and claims processing including monitoring their activities. Soon after the *Deepwater Horizon* oil spill, the Deepwater Integrated Services Team (IST)[52] was established at the direction of the National Incident Command, under the command of the U.S. Coast Guard, and initially was responsible for monitoring BP's claims process. As Deepwater IST scaled back, its responsibilities were transitioned to relevant agencies. The oversight effort for cost reimbursement and claims activities transitioned to Justice, who continues to lead the efforts. In addition, DOI and NOAA are serving as the federal government representatives for the natural resource trustees in evaluating the environmental impact of the *Deepwater Horizon* incident.

The Role of the Deepwater Integrated Services Team Evolved during the Response Effort and Concluded in February 2011

In order to coordinate federal agencies' and departments' efforts to provide support services and initially monitor claims in response to the *Deepwater Horizon* oil spill, the IST was established with the Federal Emergency Management Agency (FEMA) leading this effort. Figure 4 shows the IST participants. IST coordinated intergovernmental efforts to monitor BP and the GCCF claims processes to promote their efficiency and effectiveness by raising awareness and ensuring accountability and positive outcomes. It also helped raise awareness of concerns related to payment policy clarity for claimants, data access and reporting, and coordination of federal and state benefits and services to avoid duplicate payments. In conjunction with the stand-down of the National Incident Command on September 30, 2010, IST began scaling back its staffing and functions and concluded the final transition of its functions to federal agencies under the agencies existing authorities and responsibilities effective February 1, 2011. For example, Justice continues to monitor the effectiveness and efficiency of the BP and GCCF claims processes, and

---

[52]In response to the *Deepwater Horizon* oil spill, on May 2010 DHS's Federal Emergency Management Agency (FEMA) was tasked as the coordination lead for the Deepwater Integrated Services Team. The focus of the IST was to monitor BP's claims process and coordinate the delivery of federal programs that could provide social services and small business assistance for individuals, families, and businesses, as well as state and local government entities affected by the spill.

also leads coordination efforts to connect government stakeholders with BP and GCCF as needed.

Figure 4: Participants in the Deepwater IST

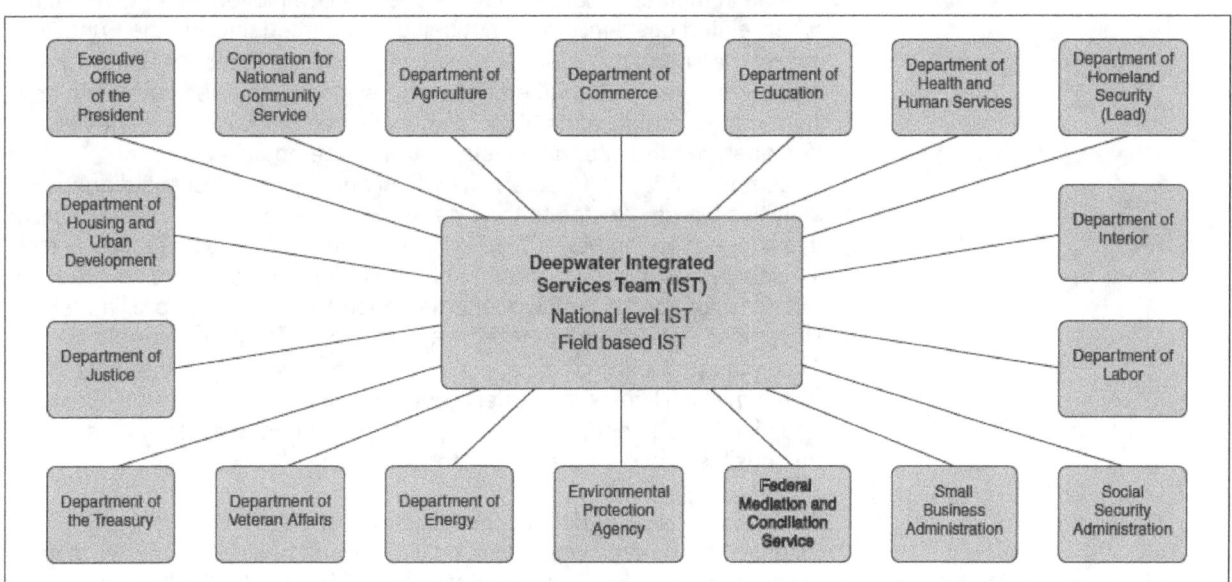

Source: Deepwater Integrated Services Team.

Justice Is Leading the Federal Government's Efforts to Monitor GCCF's Claims Process

Justice has been proactive in leading federal agencies in using a range of approaches to establish practices to monitor the cost reimbursement and claims activities of BP and the GCCF. Justice encouraged BP to establish the Trust and the GCCF. Justice sent at least four letters to GCCF highlighting key concerns with the claims process. For example, in a letter dated February 4, 2011, Justice reiterated that OPA requires BP and other responsible parties to pay for damages as a result of the oil spill and to make the GCCF claims process more transparent so that claimants clearly understand the status of their claims. According to a Justice official, Justice's involvement stems from a regulatory interest to ensure that the administration of the Trust is consistent with OPA and that claimants are treated fairly, as well as to help ensure transparency.

On another related front, in order to identify non-OPA-compensable costs which the federal government incurred due to the duration, size, and location of the *Deepwater Horizon* oil spill, OMB issued guidance between July 2010 and January 2011 to federal agencies on identifying, documenting and reporting costs associated with the *Deepwater Horizon* oil spill.[53] Specifically, OMB's guidance directed federal agencies to include in their summary cost reports federal employee time, travel, and other related costs that were not being reimbursed through the Fund.[54] Justice has used the information submitted by the federal agencies to identify and seek reimbursement from responsible parties for certain non-OPA-compensable costs. According to Justice officials, Justice reviewed and analyzed the information submitted by the agencies through December 31, 2010, to determine which agency costs reflected agency activities directly related to the *Deepwater Horizon* oil spill. After compiling this information, on May 13, 2011, Justice sent the responsible parties an invoice requesting reimbursement to the federal government for $81.6 million for the first two reporting quarters (through approximately December 2010) for other federal agency non-OPA-compensable costs.[55] According to Justice officials, they will continue to analyze the *Deepwater Horizon* oil spill costs that federal agencies submit on a quarterly basis and plan to send additional requests for cost reimbursement to the responsible parties, as appropriate.

Justice has also coordinated investigations of *Deepwater Horizon* potential fraudulent claims from individuals and businesses under review by its National Center for Disaster Fraud.[56] As of July 28, 2011, over

---

[53]OMB Memorandum M-10-29, *Identifying and Documenting Costs of Government Activities Related to the BP Deepwater Horizon Oil Spill* (July 1, 2010); OMB Management Procedures Memorandum No. 2010-35, *Reporting Costs of Government Activities Related to the BP Deepwater Horizon Oil Spill* (Oct. 5, 2010); OMB Memorandum M-11-09, *Supplemental Guidance on Reporting Costs of Government Activities Related to the BP Deepwater Horizon Oil Spill* (Jan. 12, 2011); and, OMB Memorandum M-11-09 (revised), *Supplemental Guidance on Reporting Costs of Government Activities Related to the BP Deepwater Horizon Oil Spill* (Jan. 13, 2011).

[54]Examples included NOAA serving as the lead science agency and Department of Energy evaluating methods and risks to stem the flow of oil.

[55]According to Justice officials, the $81.6 million payment will be deposited into the U.S. Treasury.

[56]The National Center for Disaster Fraud was established by the Criminal Division of the United States Department of Justice in the fall of 2005 in the wake of Hurricane Katrina. The Center is located in Baton Rouge, Louisiana. Its purpose is to receive and screen reports from the public about possible fraud relating to disasters of all types, and to refer those reports to the field offices of appropriate federal law enforcement agencies.

3,000 referrals had been submitted for investigation from BP, GCCF and NPFC.

The National Commission on BP Deepwater Horizon Oil Spill and Offshore Drilling recommended that Justice's Office of Dispute Resolution conduct an evaluation of GCCF once all claims have been paid, in order to inform claims processes in future spills of national significance. The Commission said the evaluation should include a review of the process, the guidelines used for compensation, and the success rate for avoiding lawsuits.

NPFC has also participated in monitoring the individual and business claim activities of BP and GCCF in order to determine and prepare for any potential inflows of related claims that might be coming to NPFC following any significant number of claim denials by BP or the other responsible parties. Claimants who are denied payment by the GCCF or whose claims are not settled within 90 days may pursue the following options:

- appeal GCCF's decision, if the claim is in excess of $250,000 under procedures established by the GCCF administrator;
- begin litigation against the responsible parties in court;[57] or
- file a claim with NPFC.[58]

Over 900 *Deepwater Horizon* claims (some of which were denied by BP and GCCF) have been filed with NPFC between September 2010 and May 2011. NPFC's claims adjudication division regularly obtains information from GCCF on GCCF claims paid and denied. This oversight information allows NPFC to determine the extent to which cases should be closed as the claimants were paid by GCCF, helps prevent claimants being paid by both GCCF and NPFC for the same claim, and enables it to better anticipate denied GCCF claims that could be resubmitted to NPFC for adjudication.

---

[57] Numerous individuals, businesses, states, and the federal government have begun various actions in a number of courts against several companies, including BP, seeking damages or declaratory or injunctive relief under several laws, including OPA. Many of these pending cases have been consolidated in multidistrict litigation in the U.S. District Court for the Eastern District of Louisiana. See http://www.laed.uscourts.gov/OilSpill/OilSpill.htm.

[58] If a claimant decides to commence litigation against the responsible parties, NPFC will not review the same claim until the litigation has concluded.

DOI and NOAA Are Actively Participating As the Federal Natural Resource Trustees

The natural resource trustees for the *Deepwater Horizon* incident—responsible for evaluating the oil spill's impacts on natural resources—are DOI, NOAA, DOD, and the five Gulf Coast states (Texas, Louisiana, Mississippi, Alabama, and Florida). On September 27, 2010, NOAA sent the eight responsible parties identified by DOI a Notice of Intent to Conduct Restoration Planning for the *Deepwater Horizon* incident on behalf of federal and state trustees. On April 21, 2011, the federal and state trustees announced that BP had agreed to provide $1 billion from the Trust for early restoration projects in the Gulf of Mexico to address natural resource damage caused by the *Deepwater Horizon* oil spill. Under the agreement, the $1 billion will be provided to fund projects such as the rebuilding of coastal marshes, replenishment of damaged beaches, conservation of sensitive areas for ocean habitat for injured wildlife, and restoration of barrier islands and wetlands that provide natural protection from storms.

The $1 billion in early restoration projects will be selected and implemented as follows:

- DOI will select and implement $100 million in projects;
- NOAA will select and implement $100 million in projects;
- each of the five states (Alabama, Florida, Louisiana, Mississippi, and Texas) will select and implement $100 million in projects; and
- DOI and NOAA will select projects submitted by the state trustees for $300 million.

Conclusion

Several factors contribute to financial risks that the federal government will continue to face for a number of years as a result of the *Deepwater Horizon* oil spill. Future uncertainties include the total expenses of fully addressing the impact of the *Deepwater Horizon* oil spill and the responsible parties' and guarantors' willingness and ability to continue to pay, possibly for the next several decades. Uncertainty over federal financial risks also arise from the per barrel oil tax expiration in 2017—the primary revenue source for the Fund—and the need for funding in response to other potential significant spills. Given these risks, it will be important for Congress to consider whether additional legislative action would help ensure that OPA's $1 billion per-incident cap does not hinder NPFC's ability to reimburse federal agencies' costs, pay natural resources damages, and pay valid claims submitted by individuals and businesses. To this end, we are reiterating the Matter for Congressional Consideration in our November 2010 report that Congress should consider amending OPA, or enacting new legislation to take into account reimbursements from responsible parties in calculating an incident's expenditures against the Fund's $1 billion per-incident expenditure cap.[59] For its part, NPFC has an opportunity to document and incorporate the lessons learned from its *Deepwater Horizon* oil spill experience in its policies and procedures to help improve its management of any future spills of national significance. Capturing lessons learned about processing such claims will be essential should a significant spill occur in the future In addition, NPFC took action to address recommendations made in our November 2010 report to ensure and maintain cost reimbursement policies and procedures and ensure responsible parties are properly notified (see app. I for the recommendations and their current status).

Matter for Congressional Consideration

Congress should consider the options for funding the Oil Spill Liability Trust Fund as well as the optimal level of funding to be maintained in the Fund, in light of the expiration of the Fund's per barrel tax funding source in 2017.

Recommendation for Executive Action

In order to provide guidance for responding to a spill of national significance and build on lessons learned, we recommend that the Secretary of Homeland Security direct the Director of the Coast Guard's NPFC to finalize the revisions the Coast Guard is drafting to its *Claims Adjudication Division's Standard Operating Procedures* to include specific required steps for processing claims received in the event of a spill of national significance.

Agency Comments

We provided copies of the draft report to the Departments of Homeland Security, Justice, Interior, Defense, and Commerce; Office of Management and Budget; and Environmental Protection Agency for comment prior to finalizing the report. In its written comments, reproduced in appendix VIII, the Department of Homeland Security concurred with our recommendation and stated it plans to finalize changes to operating procedures by October 31, 2011. The Departments of Homeland Security, Justice, and Interior and Environmental Protection Agency also provided technical comments that were incorporated, as appropriate.

---

[59]GAO-11-90R, 34.

We are sending copies of this report to the appropriate congressional committees. We are also sending copies to the Secretary of Homeland Security; Director of NPFC; Attorney General of the United States; Secretary of the Interior; Secretary of Defense; Secretary of Commerce; Director of Office of Management and Budget; Administrator of the Environmental Protection Agency; and to other interested parties. This report will also be available at no charge on our website at http://www.gao.gov.

Should you or your staff have any questions concerning this report, please contact Susan Ragland at (202) 512-8486 or raglands@gao.gov. Contact points for our Offices of Congressional Relations and Public Affairs may be found on the last page of this report. GAO staff who made key contributions to this report are listed in appendix IX.

Susan Ragland

Susan Ragland
Director
Financial Management and Assurance

List of Requesters

The Honorable John Conyers, Jr.
Ranking Member
Committee on the Judiciary
House of Representatives

The Honorable Bennie G. Thompson
Ranking Member
Committee on Homeland Security
House of Representatives

The Honorable Tom Carper
Chairman
Subcommittee on Federal Financial Management, Government
Information, Federal Services, and International Security
Committee on Homeland Security and Governmental Affairs
United States Senate

The Honorable Sheldon Whitehouse
Chairman
Subcommittee on Oversight
Committee on Environment and Public Works
United States Senate

The Honorable Cliff Stearns
Chairman
Subcommittee on Oversight and Investigations
Committee on Energy and Commerce
House of Representatives

The Honorable Mary Landrieu
 United States Senate

The Honorable Michael C. Burgess
The Honorable Nick J. Rahall, II
House of Representatives

Appendix I: Status of Prior Recommendations

The National Pollution Fund Center (NPFC) took actions as of September 2011 to address the four recommendations we made in our November 2010 report.[1]

Table 2: Implementation Status of Prior GAO Recommendations

GAO recommendations	Implementation status
In order to help establish and maintain effective cost reimbursement policies and procedures for the Fund, we recommended that the Secretary of Homeland Security direct the Director of the Coast Guard's NPFC to update NPFC's policies and procedures to include:	
1. Current Fund reimbursement-billing practices that reflect both a percentage of federal agencies' obligations as well as expenditures.	NPFC officials stated they updated their policies and procedures to formally incorporate the practices in April 2011.
2. Specific procedural guidance on processing Department of Defense (DOD) requests for reimbursement using Military Interdepartmental Purchase Requests.	NPFC officials stated they updated their policies and procedures to formally incorporate the procedures in April 2011.
In order to ensure that responsible parties are properly notified of their responsibilities for an oil spill, we recommend that the Secretary of Homeland Security direct the Director of NPFC to:	
3. Update NPFC's current policies to reflect current organization and structure and management's directives.	NPFC officials stated that this recommendation resulted from outdated procedures regarding Notices of Designation and the procedures were corrected in August 2011.
4. Update NPFC's current procedures to provide detailed guidance and procedures for identifying and documenting responsible party notification.	In their comments to GAO's November 2010 report, NPFC officials disagreed with our recommendation and stated its responsible party designations are unrelated to the imposition of liability under the Oil Pollution Act of 1990 (OPA) and that they serve the purpose of getting a responsible party to advertise the *Deepwater Horizon* oil spill claims process. NPFC's procedures provided that responsible parties and their guarantors are to be notified of their oil spill-related responsibilities. In accordance with its procedures, NPFC sent formal letters of designation to some, but not all, of the responsible parties it identified for the *Deepwater Horizon* oil spill. To other responsible parties, NPFC provided only invoices that reflected NPFC's assessment of liability for removal costs. NPFC's procedures for notifying responsible parties using invoices did not clearly communicate their "responsible party" designation. NPFC officials stated that NPFC updated its procedures in August 2011 to clarify the process.

Source: GAO-11-397R and GAO analysis of NPFC information.

---

[1]GAO-11-90R.

Appendix II: Objectives, Scope, and Methodology

This report is the third and final in a series of reports on the *Deepwater Horizon* oil spill in response to this request. Shortly after the explosion and subsequent sinking of BP's leased *Deepwater Horizon* oil rig in the Gulf of Mexico in April 2010, we were requested to (1) identify the financial risks to the federal government and, more specifically, to the Oil Spill Liability Trust Fund (Fund) resulting from oil spills, particularly *Deepwater Horizon*, (2) assess NPFC's internal controls for ensuring that processes and payments for cost reimbursements and processes for claims related to the *Deepwater Horizon* oil spill were appropriate, and (3) describe the extent to which the federal government oversees the BP and Gulf Coast Claims Facility (GCCF) *Deepwater Horizon* oil spill-related claims processes.

Concerning our analysis of the financial risks and exposures to the federal government and Fund, we identified and analyzed applicable laws and regulations in order to determine statutory and regulatory limitations on the liability of responsible parties that may pose financial risks to the Fund and federal government. We also considered GAO reports on the use of the Fund, reviewed publicly available quarterly financial information of responsible parties through June 2011 to gain an understanding of the extent to which contingent liabilities are reported by these companies, and reviewed reports issued by the Congressional Research Service on responsible party liabilities under OPA. [1] To determine the obligations and costs incurred in relation to the Fund's $1 billion per incident cap, we obtained and analyzed daily financial summary data NPFC used related to the *Deepwater Horizon* oil spill. We also reviewed NPFC's daily financial summary data to compare the amounts federal and state agencies had submitted for reimbursement from the Fund to the amounts NPFC had authorized for payment from the Fund to these government agencies through May 2011. We obtained invoices NPFC sent to the responsible parties to reimburse the Fund, analyzed the requests for reimbursements submitted by federal and state agencies, and compared the invoiced amounts to the amounts federal and state agencies had submitted for payment from the Fund.

To assess NPFC's internal controls for ensuring that agencies' requests for cost reimbursements and claims from individuals and businesses are

---

[1] See GAO, *Maritime Transportation: Major Oil Spills Occur Infrequently, but Risks to the Federal Oil Spill Fund Remain*, GAO-07-1085 (Washington, D.C.: Sept. 7, 2007).

appropriate, we reviewed relevant sections of OPA and compared the
sections to NPFC's cost reimbursement and claims Standard Operating
Procedures and to GAO's *Standards for Internal Control in the Federal
Government*.[2] We interviewed cognizant NPFC officials about its cost
reimbursement and claims processes, *Deepwater Horizon* oil spill
response efforts, specific cost recovery actions under way or completed,
and the NPFC division(s) responsible for those actions. We also
conducted walkthroughs of the cost reimbursement and claims
processes, observed NPFC's process for generating an invoice to the
responsible parties for *Deepwater Horizon* response costs, and
conducted a site visit to the Gulf area in October 2010.

For agency cost reimbursements, we tested a statistical sample of
payments to federal and state agencies for their *Deepwater Horizon*
removal and response activities paid from the Fund between April 2010
and April 2011. We interviewed NPFC's Case Management Officer for
Deepwater Horizon and other NPFC officials to gain a thorough
understanding of NPFC's cost reimbursement process. In addition, we
performed walk-throughs of NPFC's cost reimbursement and billing
processes and reviewed NPFC's Case Management's standard operating
procedures and other guidance documents. We also obtained updated
information from NPFC officials about the status of the response to
recommendations made in our November 2010 report.

To determine our population for sampling cost reimbursements for the
Deepwater Horizon oil spill, we obtained a disbursement file from U.S.
Coast Guard's Finance Center (FINCEN)[3] which consisted of 173,458
disbursements from the Fund between April 2010 and April 2011. We
reviewed the information in the file to determine whether we could rely on
the data in order to select a sample and test internal controls associated
with the cost reimbursement process. We assessed the reliability of the
data in the file and determined it could be used to select a statistical
sample for testing. From the population of 173,458 disbursements from
the Fund between April 2010 and April 2011, we identified 954

---

[2]GAO, *Standards for Internal Control in the Federal Government*, GAO/AIMD-00-21.3.1
(Washington, D.C.: November 1999).

[3]FINCEN is located in Chesapeake, Va., and serves as the data center for finance and
procurement, central bill paying, and financial accounting for the U.S. Coast Guard.

disbursements for *Deepwater Horizon*.[4] We then selected a random
statistical sample of 57 disbursements for testing. We tested the 57 Fund
disbursements for adherence to NPFC's case management standard
operating procedures. Our test included reviewing the request for
reimbursement submission to

- determine if a signed Pollution Removal Funding Authorization
  (PRFA) or Military Interdepartmental Purchase Request (MIPR) was
  in place between the performing federal or state agency and the
  Federal On-Scene Coordinator;
- assess that the services or goods provided were in accordance with
  the terms of the PRFA statement of work or MIPR agreement;
- confirm evidence of supporting documentation;
- confirm the Federal On-Scene Coordinator's approval of the amount
  requested for reimbursement by the performing federal or state
  agency; and
- confirm an NPFC Case Manager signed an Authorization to Pay or
  Authority to Allow Intra-Governmental Payment and Collection
  memorandum addressed to FINCEN authorizing payment from the
  Fund.

For claims, we tested a statistical sample of finalized *Deepwater Horizon*
claims presented to the Fund between September 2010 and April 2011.
First, we interviewed NPFC's Claims Division Chief, Senior Claims
Manager, and other cognizant NPFC officials to gain an understanding of
NPFC's claims adjudication process. On the basis of information provided
by NPFC, we identified 432 finalized claims from NPFC's Claims
Processing System[5] submitted for the *Deepwater Horizon* spill between
September 2010 and April 2011. From the population of 432 finalized
claims, we selected a random sample of 60 claims to test. We tested the
sample for adherence to OPA's and NPFC's claims policies and
procedures. We tested NPFC's adherence to its procedures for claim

---

[4]The 954 *Deepwater Horizon* disbursements were identified by retaining only transactions
with the *Deepwater Horizon* Federal Project Number (N10036), were expenditure-type
transactions ("EXP") and had a document ID identifying them as either a Military
Interdepartmental Purchase Request (MIPR) (doc ID "28") or Pollution Removal Funding
Authorization (PRFA) (doc ID "34") disbursement, and eliminating the Treasury
confirmations ("JE Category field"). Federal Project Numbers are unique numbers
assigned by NPFC to identify oil pollution incidents.

[5]NPFC's Claims Processing System is a work flow system that supports the initial receipt,
administrative processing, and subsequent routing and payment of claims for NPFC.

receipt, initial review, adjudication review, determination, and reconsideration. In conducting our work, we reviewed documents from individual claim files, and also used NPFC's Claims Processing System to review the responsible party's communication on the claims presented to the NPFC for payment. We tested to ensure that NPFC had a process for complying with OPA's prioritization requirement that all claims be presented to the responsible party before they can be presented to the Fund. We tested to confirm that the claims were signed and submitted in writing, for a sum certain amount, and were processed by NPFC within the required statutory time frame. Because there were no payments made for claims submitted for *Deepwater Horizon* for our scope period, we were unable to test the payment process.

Because we selected a sample of claims and cost disbursements, our results are estimates of the population and thus are subject to sample errors that are associated with samples of this size and type. Our confidence in the precision of the results from these samples is expressed in 95-percent confidence intervals. A 95-percent confidence interval is the interval that would contain the true population value in 95 percent of samples of this type and size. The results of our tests on both the sample of claims and the sample cost disbursements did not find any exceptions. On the basis of these results, we estimated that the 95-percent confidence intervals range from zero to 5 percent for both sample results and concluded with 95-percent confidence that the error rate in each population does not exceed 5 percent.

We reviewed NPFC's policies and procedures for processing and adjudicating oil spill claims and obtained information on NPFC's claims contingency planning for handling potential surges in claims submitted related to the *Deepwater Horizon* oil spill.

We obtained claims information from the GCCF and NPFC through May 2011 to describe the number and types of claims filed by individuals and businesses against the GCCF and the Fund, and the number and dollar amounts submitted, reviewed, and paid. We also obtained the Notices of Designation[6] NPFC sent to responsible parties and interviewed NPFC

---

[6]When information of an oil spill is received, the source or sources of the discharge or threat are designated where possible and appropriate. If the designated source is a vessel or facility, the responsible party and the guarantor, if known, are notified by telephone, telefax, or other rapid means of that designation. The designation will be confirmed by a written Notice of Designation.

officials about their methodology for identifying responsible parties and
their procedures for notifying them.

We interviewed officials at the Departments of Commerce, Defense,
Interior, and Homeland Security, and the Environmental Protection
Agency to obtain an understanding of these agencies' response activities
for the *Deepwater Horizon* oil spill and its process for billing on costs
incurred. We also obtained invoices NPFC sent to the responsible parties
and analyzed these billed amounts and summarized the amounts by
federal and state agencies. We compared the amounts submitted for
reimbursement from the Fund by the performing federal and state
agencies, to the amounts billed to the responsible parties on their behalf
to identify which agencies have begun their cost recovery efforts. We
compared the amounts requested for reimbursement from the Fund by
the performing federal and state agencies, to the amounts reimbursed
from the Fund to determine the status of agency's cost recovery efforts.

To describe how the federal government oversees the BP and GCCF
claims processes, we interviewed Department of Justice (Justice) officials
about their oversight of BP's claims process, the establishment of BP's
$20 billion Trust, and the setup of the GCCF. We reviewed Justice's
comments on the draft GCCF Emergency Advanced Payment and GCCF
Final Payment protocols, and we obtained and reviewed the Trust
agreement. We obtained and reviewed letters sent by Justice to the
responsible parties discussing their financial responsibilities in connection
with the *Deepwater Horizon* oil spill, which requested that the responsible
parties provide advance notice of any significant corporate actions related
to organization, structure, and financial position. We obtained and
reviewed letters sent by Justice to the GCCF highlighting concerns about
its pace for processing claims, need for transparency, and compliance
with OPA standards. In addition, we interviewed Deepwater Integrated
Services Team (IST) officials about their coordination activities regarding
the BP and GCCF claims process and social services coordination
efforts. The IST which was established in June 2010 and stood down in
September 2010, took steps to raise awareness of concerns related to
claim payment policy clarity, data access and reporting of overall claims
information, and the coordination of federal/state benefits and services to
avoid duplicate payments. We reviewed documentation from the
Deepwater IST including its coordination plan, team updates, and
transition plan. We did not evaluate the effectiveness of the monitoring
and oversight efforts by Justice and the Deepwater IST. Furthermore, we
reviewed publicly available claim reports from BP and GCCF for claim
amounts paid, but we did not test the claims data or amounts reported by

BP or GCCF. We also interviewed Office of Management and Budget and Justice officials about their role and planned actions in collecting and reviewing agency quarterly cost submissions to bill the responsible parties on behalf of the federal government.[7]

We conducted this performance audit from July 2010 to October 2011 in accordance with generally accepted government auditing standards. Those standards require that we plan and perform the audit to obtain sufficient, appropriate evidence to provide a reasonable basis for our findings and conclusions based on our audit objectives. We believe that the evidence obtained provides a reasonable basis for our findings and conclusions based on our audit objectives.

---

[7]As of May 31, 2011, Justice had sent one bill in the amount of $81.6 million for cost recovery from the responsible parties.

Appendix III: National Pollution Fund Center's Individual and Business Claims Process

Overview

OPA provides for the payment of claims for uncompensated removal costs and certain damages caused by the discharge, or substantial threat of discharge, of oil into or upon the navigable waters of the U.S., its adjoining shorelines, or the Exclusive Economic Zone of the U.S. Adjudication and payment of claims for certain uncompensated removal costs and damages are paid out of the Principal Fund of the Fund.

Order of Presentment and Time Limitation for Submitting Claims to NPFC. Claims for removal or damages may be presented first to the Fund only in the following situations: NPFC has advertised or notified claimants in writing; by a responsible party who may assert a claim; by a governor of a state for removal costs incurred by the state;[1] and by a U.S. claimant in a case where a foreign offshore unit has discharged oil causing damage for which the Fund is liable.

In all other cases where the source of the discharge can be identified, the claimant must first present their OPA claim to the responsible party for payment. If the responsible party denies the claim the claimant may submit the claim to NPFC for adjudication. Regardless of specific action to deny the claim, if the responsible party is unable or unwilling to pay the claim within 90 days of the claimant's submission, the claimant may then submit the claim to NPFC for adjudication. If the responsible party denies a claim that is subsequently processed and payment is made from the Fund, NPFC will seek to recover these costs from the responsible party. Damage claims must be made within 3 years of when the damage and its connection to the spill were reasonably discoverable with the exercise of due care. Claims for removal costs must be made within 6 years after the date of completion of all removal actions for the incident.[2]

Designation of the Source of the Incident, Responsible Party Notification, and Advertisement. The process of designating the source of an oil discharge and notifying the responsible party frequently advances concurrently with the Federal On-Scene Coordinator's attempt to identify the responsible party during the initial stages of spill response. In addition

---

[1]To facilitate providing states with funds quickly for their oil spill response costs, NPFC has developed an expedited claims procedure for state governments.

[2]Date of completion of all removal actions is defined as the actual date of completion of all removal actions for the incident or the date the Federal On-Scene Coordinator determines that the removal actions which form the basis for the costs being claimed are completed, whichever is earlier.

to the Federal On-Scene Coordinator issuing a letter of Federal Interest,[3] the Federal On-Scene Coordinator and NPFC's Case Management and Claims Division[4] may decide that the potential for claims exists. Once decided, the Claim Manager is normally responsible for executing the Notice of Designation.[5] Designation of a responsible party may also occur immediately following an on-site visit or more incrementally as information on the identity of the responsible party becomes available.

Claimant Requirements. While NPFC has a form which claimants may use to submit their claim, there is no required format for submitting a claim to NPFC. However, OPA through its implementing regulations, requires that the claim be (1) submitted in writing, (2) for a sum certain amount of compensation for each category of uncompensated damages or removal, and (3) signed by the claimant. The claimant bears the burden of providing all evidence, information, and documentation deemed necessary by NPFC to support the claim. While the claim is pending against the Fund, if the claimant receives any compensation for the claimed amounts, the claimant is required to immediately amend the claim submitted to NPFC.

---

[3]Letters of Federal Interest are issued by the Federal On-Scene Coordinator to assert the need for positive responsible party action.

[4]NPFC's Case Management Division is responsible for providing access to the Emergency Fund for Federal removal costs and for accurate cost documentation to support cost recovery. NPFC's Claims Adjudication Division is responsible for providing assistance to the victims of oil spills by receiving, processing, adjudicating, settling, and approving the payment of OPA claims. It is also responsible for advertising for claims if the responsible party does not.

[5]To begin the claims process, 33 U.S.C. 2714 provides that once an incident becomes known, the source or sources of a discharge or threat shall be designated where possible and appropriate. And, if the designated source is a vessel or a facility, the responsible party and the guarantor, if known, shall be immediately notified of the designation. "Designation" is an OPA term used in connection with the initiation of the claims process and is aimed at the advertisement of responsible party responsibility to potential claimants.

Table 3: List of OPA-Compensable Claim Types/Description, Eligibility, and NPFC Claims Division Responsible for Processing the Claim

Claim type	Description	Eligible claimant	Responsible NPFC claims division
Natural Resource Damages	Damages for injury to, destruction of, or loss of natural resources, including the reasonable costs of assessing the damage.	Federal, state, foreign and Indian tr bal trustees.	Natural Resource Damage Claims Division
Real or Personal Property	Damages or economic loss related to the destruction or harm of real or personal property presented by either a claimant owning or leasing the property. Does not include personal injury.	Person or entity who owns or leases property.	Claims Adjudication Division
Removal Costs[a]	Costs to prevent, minimize, or mitigate oil pollution.	Anyone incurring removal costs.	Claims Adjudication Division
Loss of Subsistence Use of Natural Resources	Damages resulting from the injury, destruction, or loss of natural resources used by the claimant to obtain food, shelter, clothing, medicine, or other minimum necessities of life.[b]	Claimant who actually uses for subsistence, the natural resources which have been injured, destroyed, or lost, without regard to the ownership or management of the resources.	Natural Resource Damage Claims Division
Loss of Government Revenues	Net loss of taxes, royalties, rents, fees, or net profit shares due to the injury, destruction, or loss of real property, personal property, or natural resources.	Federal government, state, or a political subdivision of a state.	Claims Adjudication Division
Loss of Profits and Earning Capacity	Damages equal to the loss of profits or impairment of earning capacity due to the injury, destruction, or loss of property or natural resources.	Claimant sustaining the loss or impairment.	Claims Adjudication Division
Cost of Increased Public Services	Net costs of providing increased or additional public services during or after removal activities, including protection from fire, safety, or health hazards caused by a discharge of oil.	State or political subdivsion of a state.	Claims Adjudication Division
Claims by a Responsible Party	Claims submitted by a responsible party are not processed like other OPA claims. A responsible party may present a complete defense or limitation of liability claim to NPFC for removal costs and damages paid under the provisions of OPA. Claims that meet the initial review and preliminary screening must first be evaluated to determine "entitlement" to a complete defense or limit of liability. Once entitlement has been granted, the underlying cost portion of the claim may be measured and adjudicated.	Responsible party who establishes entitlement to a defense to liability or limitation of liability in accordance with OPA (33 U.S.C. 2703-04 and 2708).	Claims Adjudication Division

Source: GAO analysis of NPFC information.

[a]Claimant must establish that the actions taken were necessary, removal costs were incurred as a result of these actions, and the actions taken were determined by the Federal On-Scene Coordinator to be consistent with the National Contingency Plan or were directed by the Federal On-Scene Coordinator. This is the most common claim type received by NPFC.

[b]Compensation allowable is based on the reasonable replacement cost of the natural resource needed during the loss period for subsistence, less all compensation made available for subsistence loss, all income received by using the time otherwise for subsistence, and all overhead or other normal expenses for subsistence use that was avoided as a result of the incident.

NPFC's Claims Process. NPFC has established standard operating procedures[6] for the activities its Claims Division undertakes throughout its process for receiving and adjudicating claims. For some oil spill incidents, the Claims Division activities begin prior to the submission of any claims. These activities include designation of the source of the spill, responsible party notification, advertisement, as well as a number of on-site activities. As noted in the table above, the Claims Adjudication Division accepts claims for uncompensated removal costs incurred and damages suffered as a result of an oil pollution incident, whereas the Natural Resource Damage Claims Division[7] accepts claims from authorized claimants for damages to natural resources and loss of subsistence use claims. In general, regardless of which division is responsible for adjudicating the claim, NPFC follows the same steps in processing these claims. [8]

1. Claim Receipt and Assignment
2. Initial Review
3. Adjudication Review
4. Determination and Reconsideration
5. Payment
6. Archive

---

[6]U.S. Coast Guard, NPFC, *Standard Operating Procedures of the Claims Adjudication Division*, NPFCINST M16451.21 (April 2004).

[7]NPFC's Natural Resource Damage Claims Division adjudicates claims for natural resource damages arising out of oil spills (or the substantial threat of a spill) to the navigable waters of the United States. Those damages may include the cost to restore, rehabilitate, replace, or acquire the equivalent of the injured resource; any interim lost use or diminution in value of the injured resource pending restoration; and, the reasonable cost of assessing those damages.

[8]A major difference between NPFC's Natural Resource Damage Claims Division and its Claims Adjudication Division is that the Natural Resource Damage Claims Division establishes Interagency Agreements between NPFC and the Federal Natural Resource Damage Trustees to fund initiation of natural resource damage assessments, whereas the Claims Adjudication Division does not.

Figure 5: NPFC's Claims Adjudication Process

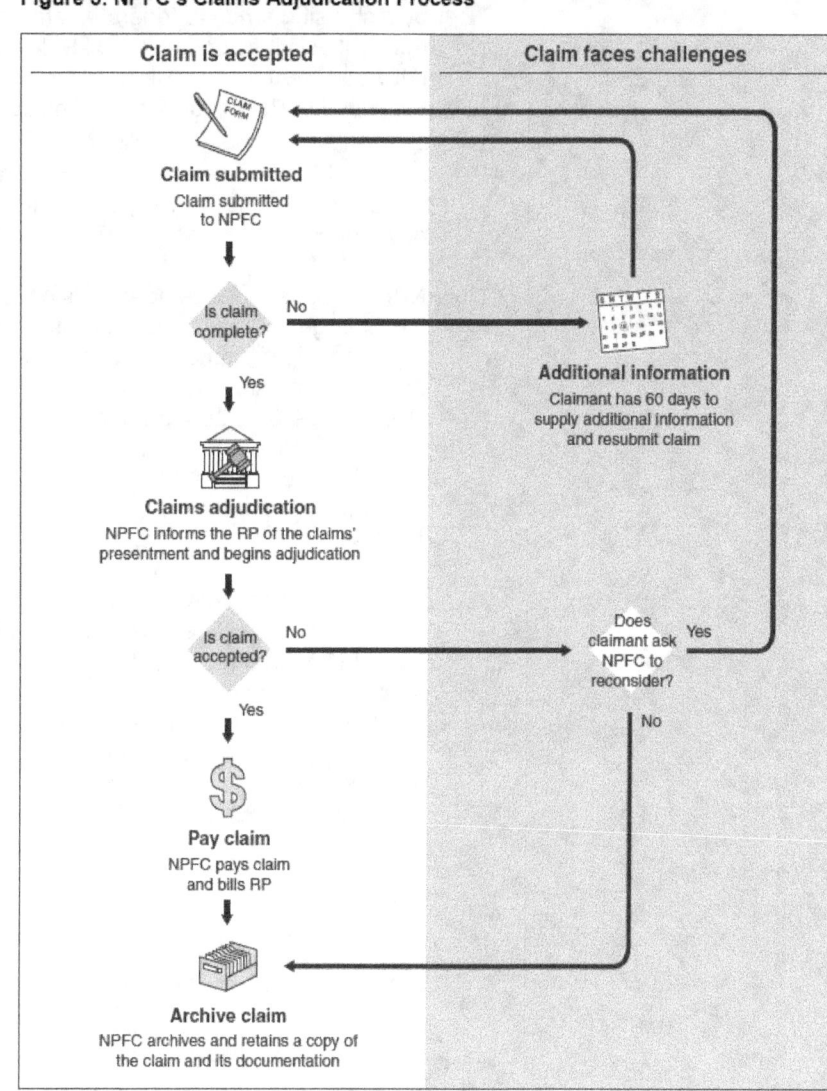

Source: GAO analysis of NPFC's Claims Adjudication Process.

Appendix IV: National Pollution Fund Center's Cost Reimbursement Process

Overview	Among other duties, the U.S. Coast Guard's NPFC administers the Fund by disbursing funds to federal, state, local, or tribal agencies for their removal activities under the Oil Pollution Act of 1990, as amended (OPA).[1] When an oil spill occurs, relevant federal agencies are notified by the National Response Center[2] including the U.S. Coast Guard and the Environmental Protection Agency (EPA).[3] The Coast Guard has responsibility and serves as the Federal On-Scene Coordinator for spills occurring in the coastal zones, while EPA has responsibility for spills that occur on land.

NPFC's Case Management Division is responsible for providing access to the Emergency Fund when a spill occurs and for working with the Federal On-Scene Coordinator and agencies to ensure accurate cost documentation to support cost recovery. NPFC's Case Management Division operates through a matrix organization comprised of four regional case teams. Each regional case team consists of a manager and multiple case officers. When a spill occurs, NPFC assigns responsibility to the regional case team representing the geographic area in which the spill occurs.

NPFC uses a three-level system to help determine the complexity of an oil spill case and its required documentation for cost reimbursement. Level I (Routine) represents about 85 percent of all oil spill incidents, in which total removal costs to the government are not expected to exceed $50,000, removal activities are localized, and removal activities can be completed within 2 weeks. For a Level I incident, agencies submit documentation to the Federal On-Scene Coordinator at the completion of removal activities. Level II (Moderately Complex) represents about 10 to

---

[1]Private companies, contractors, and other nongovernmental entities may also be part of a coordinated spill response. Contractors performing response or removal actions on behalf of the Federal On-Scene Coordinator are eligible to receive reimbursement from the Fund. However, since the *Deepwater Horizon* response efforts predominantly have involved federal and state governmental entities, this cost reimbursement appendix will focus on the process for reimbursing government agencies.

[2]The National Response Center, located at U.S. Coast Guard Headquarters, is the national communications center, continuously manned for handling activities related to response actions. The Center acts as the single point of contact for all pollution incident reporting.

[3]The National Contingency Plan requires that oil releases are reported to the National Response Center, which is staffed by the Coast Guard.

15 percent of all oil spill incidents, in which total removal costs to the government are not expected to exceed $200,000. Level II removal activities take place in multiple locations, require the involvement of several external resources (i.e., state agencies and other government units), and removal activities take longer than 2 weeks to complete. Level III (Significantly Complex) represents less than 5 percent of all oil spill incidents with total removal costs greater than $200,000. Level III removal activities take place in multiple locations, require the involvement of numerous contractors, and similar to Level II, the assistance of several external resources is needed. For both Level II and III incidents, documentation is submitted to the Federal On-Scene Coordinator as often as practical (daily if possible) until final removal activities are completed. Because the Federal On-Scene Coordinator is considered the best judge of factors regarding the oil spill, he or she is expected to select the level of documentation appropriate for the situation.

The Federal On-Scene Coordinator is responsible for issuing PRFAs or MIPRs to obtain removal and logistical services from other government agencies.

The PRFA commits the Fund to payment, by reimbursement, of costs incurred for agreed-upon pollution response activities undertaken by a federal agency assisting the Federal On-Scene Coordinator. The terms of a PRFA may include (1) salary costs, (2) travel and per diem expenses, (3) charges for the utilization of agency-owned equipment or facilities, and (4) expenses for contractor- or vendor-supplied goods or services obtained by the agency for removal assistance. Similarly, the Federal On-Scene Coordinator may issue a MIPR for agreed-upon activities of the DOD or its related components. In contrast to PRFAs, MIPRs (used primarily by DOD and its components)[4] commit the Fund to reimburse costs based on valid obligations incurred for oil spill response activities prior to being incurred. For the *Deepwater Horizon* oil spill, NPFC's cost reimbursement documentation requirements are the same for both MIPRs and PRFAs. Differences between PRFAs and MIPRs include that PRFAs are a reimbursement agreement and require the agency to submit documentation demonstrating services and have the Federal On-Scene Coordinator certify completion of work, prior to NPFC disbursing funds to the agency. For other than *Deepwater Horizon*, MIPRs allow DOD to

---

[4]DOD uses MIPRs in order to obtain and provide services to agencies.

receive the funds from NPFC prior to submitting documentation or obtaining certification of completion of work.

The following are the six major steps for NPFC's cost reimbursement process for federal, state, and local government agencies requesting payment from the Fund.

1. Federal On-Scene Coordinator issues PRFA or MIPR to government agency.
2. Government agency performs oil spill removal and response activities and submits reimbursement request to the Federal On-Scene Coordinator.
3. Federal On-Scene Coordinator reviews and certifies that services were provided by the government agency.
4. Federal On-Scene Coordinator forwards agency's reimbursement request to NPFC for review and approval.
5. NPFC reviews agency's reimbursement documentation and sends Authorization-to-Pay memorandum to FINCEN[5] approving payment from the Fund.
6. FINCEN reimburses government agency for its oil spill removal costs.

---

[5]FINCEN is located in Chesapeake, Va., and serves as the data center for finance and procurement, central bill paying, and financial accounting for the U.S. Coast Guard.

Figure 6: NPFC's Cost Reimbursement Process

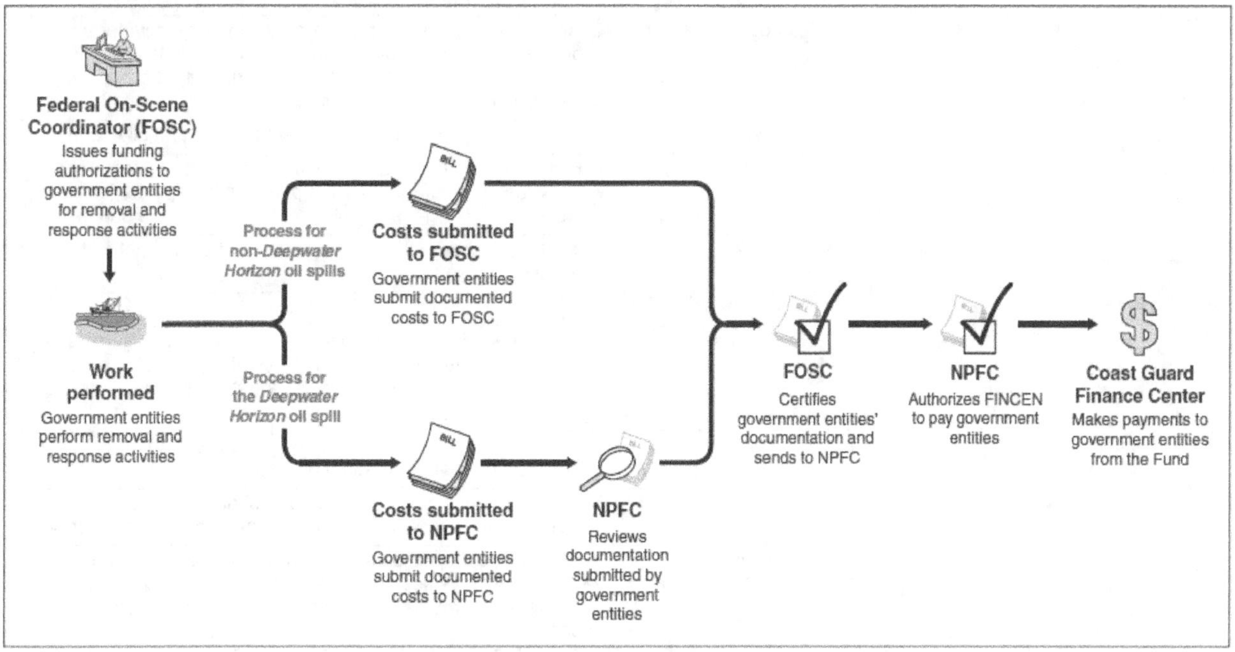

Source: GAO analysis of Cost Reimbursement Process.

Appendix V: Types of Oil Pollution Act-Compensable Removal Costs and Damages

Removal costs	
Removal of oil	Costs for the containment and removal of oil from water and shorelines including contract services (such as cleanup contractors and incident management support) and the equipment used for removal.
Disposal	Costs for the proper disposal of recovered oil and oily debris.
Personnel	Costs for government personnel and temporary government employees hired for the duration of the spill response, including costs for monitoring the activities of the responsible parties.
Prevention	Costs for the prevention or minimization of a substantial threat of an oil spill.
Damages	
Natural resources	Federal, state, foreign, or Indian tribe trustees can claim damages for injury to, or destruction of, and loss of, or loss of use of, natural resources, including the reasonable costs of assessing the damage.
Real or personal property	Damages for injury to, or economic loses resulting from destruction of, real or personal property.
Subsistence use	Damages for loss of subsistence use of natural resources, without regard to the ownership or management of the resources.
Government revenues, profits, and earning capacity	The federal, state, or local government can claim damages for the loss of taxes, royalties, rents, fees, or profits. Companies can claim damages for loss of profits or impairment of earning capacity.
Public services	States and local governments can recover costs for providing increased public services during or after an oil spill response, including protection from fire, safety, or heath hazards.

Source: GAO summary of the Oil Pollution Act of 1990 (33 U.S.C. 2702 (b)).

Appendix VI: Inspectors General Are Reviewing Agencies' *Deepwater Horizon* Oil Spill Costs

DHS, EPA, and the Department of Commerce inspectors general (IG) performed or are performing work related to their agency's costs to respond to the *Deepwater Horizon* oil spill. The DHS IG is performing an audit to determine whether the Coast Guard has adequate policies, procedures, and controls in place to capture all direct and indirect costs associated with the *Deepwater Horizon* oil spill. The EPA IG is conducting work to determine if EPA has adequate controls in place to recover its Gulf Coast oil spill response costs.

The Department of Commerce IG has published a review of the National Oceanic and Atmospheric Administration's (NOAA) tracking of oil spill costs.[1] In December 2010, the Department of Commerce IG found that while NOAA had developed processes to track the costs associated with its *Deepwater Horizon* oil spill activities, improvements are needed to ensure that all costs charged to oil spill projects—whether funded by appropriations or reimbursements—are properly recorded in the financial system and supported by sufficient, appropriate documentation. NOAA's official comments emphasized the unprecedented mobilization as a result of the scope of the *Deepwater Horizon* oil spill, and stated that as NOAA's participation has become more routine, its documentation of the oil spill activities has become more consistent. In addition, as NOAA evaluates its own execution of the response process, NOAA stated it will examine the observations provided by the IG.

---

[1]Department of Commerce Inspector General, Final Memorandum No. OIG-11-016-M *Survey of National Oceanic and Atmospheric Administration's (NOAA) System and Processes for Tracking Oil Spill Costs* (December 2010).

Appendix VII: Agencies Authorized and Reimbursed Costs for *Deepwater Horizon* Oil Spill Response Efforts

To determine the extent to which government agencies have been reimbursed from the Fund for their *Deepwater Horizon* response efforts, we obtained and analyzed reimbursement information from NPFC from April 2010 through May 2011. We found that the total maximum amount authorized through intergovernmental agency agreements for federal agencies' and states' *Deepwater Horizon* oil spill response costs is over $477.7 million. However, only seven federal agencies[1] have submitted and received payment from the Fund totaling $189.4 million for their response costs; and six federal agencies[2] that have an agreement in place authorizing them to perform work and receive reimbursement from the Fund for their response efforts, have either not yet submitted a request for reimbursement or have not provided sufficient supporting documentation for their request. (See table 4.)

Table 4: Agencies' *Deepwater Horizon* Authorized Response Costs and Reimbursements Received as of May 31, 2011

Agency	Amount authorized (ceiling amount)	Amount reimbursed (actual expenditures)	Amount reimbursed to amount authorized
Department of Defense	$163,700,489	$98,125,651	60%
Department of Interior	93,367,928	11,743,756	13%
Department of Commerce	76,962,059	25,437,859	33%
Environmental Protection Agency	61,920,863	36,002,465	58%
States[a]	40,320,984	29,854,662	74%
Department of Homeland Security	16,998,513	11,949,732	70%
Department of Energy	9,056,712	4,301,033	47%
Department of Health and Human Services	8,849,859	-	0%
Department of Labor	3,260,663	-	0%
Department of Agriculture	3,083,929	1,862,479	60%

[1]The seven federal agencies that have been reimbursed from the Fund are the Departments of Defense, Interior, Commerce, Homeland Security, Energy, Agriculture, and the Environmental Protection Agency.

[2]The six federal agencies that have intergovernmental agreements in place, but have not been paid from the Fund, are the Departments of Health and Human Services, Labor, Justice, the National Transportation Safety Board, National Security Agency, and the Office of the Director of National Intelligence.

Agency	Amount authorized (ceiling amount)	Amount reimbursed (actual expenditures)	Amount reimbursed to amount authorized
Department of Justice	141,680	-	0%
National Transportation Safety Board	24,640	-	0%
National Security Agency	18,480	-	0%
Office of the Director of National Intelligence	12,320	-	0%
Total	$477,719,119	$219,277,637	46%

Source: GAO analysis of NPFC-provided information.

[a]The amount shown for states does include amounts for certain localities that represent less than 1 percent of the total.

Appendix VIII: Comments from the Department of Homeland Security

U. S. Department of Homeland Security
Washington, D.C. 20528

Homeland Security

October 12, 2011

Susan Ragland
Director, Financial Management and Assurance
U.S. Government Accountability Office
441 G Street, NW
Washington, DC 20548

Re: Draft Report GAO-12-86, "DEEPWATER HORIZON OIL SPILL: Actions Needed to Reduce Evolving, But Uncertain Federal Financial Risks"

Dear Ms. Ragland:

Thank you for the opportunity to review and comment on this draft report. The U.S. Department of Homeland Security (DHS) appreciates the U.S. Government Accountability Office's (GAO's) work in planning and conducting its review and issuing this report.

The Department is pleased to note the report's positive acknowledgement that the United States Coast Guard (USCG) had effective internal controls in place for *Deepwater Horizon* claims processing and cost reimbursements. Specifically, controls related to documentation, review, and adjudication of individual and business claims processed and costs reimbursed following the *Deepwater Horizon* oil spill were appropriate and properly documented. The report also recognizes USCGs actions taken to address recommendations made in a previous GAO report,[1] related to issues discussed in this draft report.

The draft report contained one recommendation directed to DHS, with which the Department concurs. Specifically, GAO recommended that the Secretary of Homeland Security direct the Director of the Coast Guard's National Pollution Funds Center (NPFC) to:

Recommendation: Finalize the revisions its drafting to its *Claims Adjudication Division's Standard Operating Procedures* to include specific required steps for processing claims received in the event of a spill of national significance incident.

Response: Concur. NPFC will finalize revisions to the *Claims Adjudication Division Standard Operating Procedures* to include specifically required steps for processing claims received in the event of a spill of national significance by October 31, 2011.

---

[1] GAO, Deepwater Horizon Oil Spill: Preliminary Assessment of Federal Financial Risks and Cost Reimbursement and Notification Policies and Procedures, GAO-11-90R (Washington, DC.: Nov. 12, 2010).

Again, thank you for the opportunity to review and comment on this draft report. Technical comments were provided under separate cover. We look forward to working with you on future Homeland Security issues.

Sincerely,

Jim H. Crumpacker
Director
Departmental GAO-OIG Liaison Office

2

Appendix IX: GAO Contact and Staff Acknowledgments

GAO Contact	Susan Ragland, (202) 512-8486 or raglands@gao.gov
Staff Acknowledgments	In addition to the contact named above, Kim McGatlin (Assistant Director); F. Abe Dymond (Assistant Director); James Ratzenberger (Assistant Director); Hannah Laufe (Assistant General Counsel); Katherine Lenane (Assistant General Counsel); Jacquelyn Hamilton (Acting Assistant General Counsel); Jehan Abdel-Gawad; James Ashley; Mark Cheung; Patrick Frey; Wilfred Holloway; Donald Holzinger; David Hooper; Mark Kaufman; Jason Kelly; Matthew Latour; Chari Nash-Cannaday; Donell Ries; and Doris Yanger made significant contributions to this report.

Related GAO Products

Deepwater Horizon Oil Spill: Update on Federal Financial Risks and Claims Processing. GAO-11-397R. Washington D.C.: April 18, 2011.

Deepwater Horizon Oil Spill: Preliminary Assessment of Federal Financial Risks and Cost Reimbursement and Notification Policies and Procedures. GAO-11-90R. Washington D.C.: November 12, 2010.

Oil Spills: Cost of Major Spills May Impact Viability of Oil Spill Liability Trust Fund. GAO-10-795T. Washington D.C.: June 16, 2010.

Maritime Transportation: Major Oil Spills Occur Infrequently, but Risks Remain. GAO-08-357T. Washington D.C.: December 18, 2007.

Maritime Transportation: Major Oil Spills Occur Infrequently, but Risks to the Federal Oil Spill Fund Remain. GAO-07-1085. Washington D.C.: September 7, 2007.

U.S. Coast Guard National Pollution Funds Center: Improvements Are Needed in Internal Control Over Disbursements. GAO-04-340R. Washington D.C.: January 13, 2004.

U.S. Coast Guard National Pollution Funds Center: Claims Payment Process Was Functioning Effectively, but Additional Controls Are Needed to Reduce the Risk of Improper Payments. GAO-04-114R. Washington D.C.: October 3, 2003.

www.ingramcontent.com/pod-product-compliance
Lightning Source LLC
Chambersburg PA
CBHW082150290526
45794CB00008B/3241